£9.99

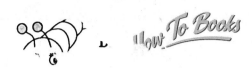

Managing
Performance
Reviews

D0318545

BISHOP AUCKLAND COLLEGE
LEARNING RESOURCE LIBRARY
ACCESSION NO. 202977
CLASS NO. 658·3123

Books to change your life and work
Our books are designed to help people achieve their goals and acquire new skills.
They are accessible, easy to read and easy to act on.
How To Books – clear, practical and encouraging books to help people take up
opportunities and meet everyday challenges. Other titles in the series include:

Managing Individual Performance
A systematic, seven step approach to enhancing employee performance and results

Investing in People
How to help your organisation achieve higher standards and a competitive edge

Managing Meetings
How to prepare, how to take part and how to follow up

Starting to Manage
How to prepare yourself for a more responsible role at work

Recruiting for Results
How to hire good performers who will help grow the business

Conducting Effective Interviews
How to find out what you need to know and achieve the right results

The *How To Series* now contains
around 200 titles in the following categories:

Business & Management
Computer Basics
General Reference
Jobs & Careers
Living & Working Abroad
Personal Finance
Self-Development
Small Business
Student Handbooks
Successful Writing

For full details, please send to our distributors for a free copy of the latest
catalogue:

How To Books
Customers Services Dept.
Plymbridge Distributors Ltd, Estover Road
Plymouth PL6 7PZ, United Kingdom
Tel: 01752 202301   Fax: 01752 202331
http://www.howtobooks.co.uk

Managing
Performance
Reviews

How to ensure your appraisals improve individual performance and organisational results

NIGEL HUNT

4th edition

How To Books

Author's dedication
To my parents, Beryl and Charles

Published by How To Books Ltd, 3 Newtec Place,
Magdalen Road, Oxford OX4 1RE, United Kingdom.
Tel: (01865) 793806. Fax: (01865) 248780.
email: info@howtobooks.co.uk
http://www.howtobooks.co.uk

All rights reserved. No part of this work may be reproduced
or stored in an information retrieval system (except for short
extracts for the purposes of review) without the express
permission of the Publishers in writing.

© Copyright 1999 Nigel Hunt

British Library Cataloguing in Publication Data
A catalogue record for this book is available from
the British Library

First published 1992
Second edition 1994
Third edition 1997
Fourth edition 1999

Cover design by Shireen Nathoo Design
Cover image by PhotoDisc

Produced for How To Books by Deer Park Productions
Typeset by Kestrel Data, Exeter
Printed and bound in Great Britain by Cromwell Press Ltd,
Trowbridge, Wiltshire

NOTE: The material contained in this book is set out in good
faith for general guidance and no liability can be accepted
for loss or expense incurred as a result of relying in particular
circumstances on statements made in the book. The laws and
regulations are complex and liable to change, and readers should
check the current position with the relevant authorities before
making personal arrangements.

Contents

List of Illustrations

Preface
to the Fourth Edition

Recent years continue to see the development of increasingly sophisticated performance review systems in all kinds of organisations, from small private enterprises to large public sector organisations. Employers recognise that effective performance review increases the job satisfaction of employees and increases organisational success.

This new edition of a book first published in 1992 as *How to Conduct Staff Appraisals* retains the structure of the earlier editions, but has undergone a change in terminology to reflect current practice in the area, and to include new developments.

Performance review is an expanding field, with more people being reviewed across a wider range of organisations. This will hopefully lead to more effective and fairer reviews; but no matter how good the system, if it isn't implemented effectively, then it is of little value. The present climate is one that does not accept inequities, does not allow discrimination. In the light of this it is important that performance review systems are effective and are implemented appropriately across organisations. In order to ensure that this occurs, systems should be reviewed and revised continually for the benefit of both the individual employee and the organisation.

This book is intended to provide a set of general guidelines for people involved in performance review, whether as reviewers or system developers. It is not meant to be prescriptive, it is not a blueprint for an ideal review system – there is no such thing. The book does offer a set of principles for good practice, which if used with care and adapted appropriately for your own organisational needs should help ensure a fair and effective performance review system.

Dr Nigel Hunt

1

Introducing Performance Review

This chapter will outline the objectives of the book and consider:

- Why you should review performance.
- Who should be reviewed.
- How and when you should review performance.
- Ethical factors.
- The role of psychological testing, counselling and negotiation in performance review.

In this book, were going to look at an easier way of interviewing. We cant go back and we cant jump *ahead* to watch people on the job for which they are being considered as a candidate.

But we can come pretty close.

LOOKING AT ORGANISATIONS AND PERFORMANCE REVIEW

An organisation's most important resource is its people. This may be a truism, but is no less valid for that. **Performance reviews** or appraisal systems should communicate the needs of both the individual and the organisation.

Performance review can be defined in different ways. The definition used here is that it is based upon a **structured interview** that requires communication between the organisation (represented by you, the **reviewer** or **appraiser**) and the individual employee (the **employee** or **appraisee**) to make assessments about the future. But performance review is more than just an interview; it is more broad-ranging, encompassing situations from setting performance objectives to counselling to selecting staff for promotion, transfer and training. Effective performance review cannot just be a once-a-year exercise. It is a continuous activity, with day-to-day communication between you and the employee.

In the formal performance review interview, neither party

should be hearing anything for the first time; problems should be addressed as and when they arise. If they are left until the performance review interview itself, they could develop from a minor problem – such as two individuals in conflict over a particular issue – to a major one where the conflict has dragged in other individuals and affected morale and productivity. If a performance review is carried out as a once-a-year exercise rather than as a continuous activity, problems stemming from several months before may have become insoluble.

There is also the problem that an annual performance review will focus largely on what has happened in the last couple of months, largely ignoring the other ten months of the year.

Performance reviews are characteristically inefficient for a number of reasons. These include:

- an unclear definition of the reviewee's job
- unclear objectives
- one or both parties being unaware of the format and aims of the interview
- untrained reviewer and/or reviewee
- subjectivity
- biased or incomplete data.

This book attempts to address these issues in order to enable the employer to set up a performance review system that is cost-effective to both the organisation and the employee, maximising **organisational cohesion, employee productivity** and **individual job satisfaction**.

It is important that the organisation has a coherent performance review, and that all employees are reviewed using the same system. Clearly, particular interviews will differ according to both the purposes of the performance review and the status of the individuals taking part, but they should all be based on the same general system so that comparisons can be made. A hotch-potch of reviews within the organisation is not cost-effective, may lead to discord and doesn't allow internal comparisons to be made.

The essential reason for a performance review system is to ensure that the right person is in the right job, remains in it and is satisfied with their work. Maximising compatibility of person and job leads to:

- maximising personal job satisfaction

- maximising performance or output.

In other words, there will be a happier, more productive work-force, which is clearly of benefit to all parties concerned.

Considering what is wrong with performance review

There are many potential problems with performance reviews. They are often poorly designed, over-ambitious and inadequately resourced, use untrained staff, and have vague aims and objectives. Too often they consist simply of unstructured interviews, with neither reviewer nor reviewee being fully aware of the purposes of the interview.

In these circumstances there is little point in carrying out the review, as very little or no useful information will be gained from it. If the interview has no direction, no purpose, then how can either party expect to achieve anything? If this type of performance review is the norm, the organisation may stop formal reviews altogether because they see little benefit to be gained from them. They would be right to do this, but at the same time they would be losing their best opportunity of fulfilling the potential of their human resources.

Producing an effective system

A performance review system should incorporate a number of elements for it to be effective. What follows is an attempt to describe them. This book will *not* provide a blueprint which, if followed to the letter, will ensure effective and valid performance reviews; individuals and organisations differ too much for that. Nevertheless, you will be led through a series of steps that, if followed in general terms, should produce an effective system. This book should be seen as a set of guidelines which, when designing your own performance review system and acting as reviewer, you should follow but will need to reinterpret for your own particular circumstances.

Understanding the need to be objective

A good performance review system has to take into account the needs and wishes of both the individuals being reviewed and the organisation for which they work. There is a strong need for objectivity and lack of bias in the collection of data to be used for discussion within a well-structured performance review interview. Too often the characteristics and requirements of the job are not known by you, the person doing the reviewing. How can you judge the effectiveness of a reviewee when you do not properly understand the job itself?

CONSIDERING WHY YOU SHOULD REVIEW PERFORMANCE

Understanding the employer's viewpoint

Performance reviews are carried out for a number of reasons. Well designed, they will help the organisation to determine:

- individual objectives
- how well objectives are being attained
- who should be promoted or transferred
- who should be considered for advancement
- who needs training and of what sort
- what jobs/tasks are actually being done
- the needs of employees.

Understanding the employee's viewpoint

The employee, though accepting the above aims, may see the performance review as having a different purpose. Unfortunately, the review so often seems something to be feared. Reviewees sometimes feel that it is carried out in order to find out who to dismiss. **This should never be the case.** If the review interview is well designed, the individual should see it as a:

- career development exercise
- way of assessing career and other wishes and needs, and how the organisation can provide them
- way of clarifying the job (duties, objectives, etc.)
- way of becoming aware of their own potential, and how that potential can be fulfilled.

This last objective may lead to difficulties if the organisation cannot fulfil this potential, because the individual, if dissatisfied, may go elsewhere. But this can be beneficial for both parties;

the reviewee may obtain greater job satisfaction by moving to another organisation, and the organisation doesn't want dissatisfied individuals on its staff. Such staff may perform poorly and demotivate others within the organisation.

The needs of the organisation and of the individual in performance review need not be incompatible. If the individuals are happy working within the organisation, they are more likely to share some of that organisation's philosophy from the organisation's need to maximise profits, to everyone having the best chance to fulfil their personal potential.

Objections to performance review

The review is often seen as a chore, something ordered from above, to be got out of the way as quickly as possible each year. This is an unfortunate attitude. The manager who holds this opinion may claim that performance review is carried out on a day-to-day informal basis, that problems which emerge are solved as they arise, suitability for promotion or a bonus are assessed using informal continuous assessment, etc. These managers will claim that formal reviews are pointless as they do not provide any information not already obtained by day-to-day contact.

There are other reasons why some managers are against reviews, or do not like doing them, including:

- dislike of the interview situation
- lack of time
- confrontational nature of the interview
- embarrassment if the reviewee is substandard
- hard work preparing for the interview
- not knowing how to structure the interview
- thinking they can't make accurate assessments of people
- difficulty fulfilling promises to employees.

This list isn't comprehensive. Most people could probably add other personal reasons for avoiding review interviews.

This book should allay the fears of managers who have lists such as the one above in their minds. If the review interview is designed properly, if both you and the employee understand the purposes and plan of the interview, if clear guidelines are given for assessing the reviewee, then perhaps managers will take a more positive attitude to performance review. The purpose of this book is to allay the fears and quieten the protests of managers who, for one reason or another, are against performance review. If both parties are made fully aware of the benefits of performance review, then the traditional notion of the review interview as a regular chore can be eliminated and replaced with a more positive attitude.

KNOWING WHO SHOULD BE REVIEWED

Many organisations only review individuals in the middle ranks. That is, they don't review lower grade office staff and blue collar workers, nor their top managers or directors. One reason is that there often exists a set format for the performance review, and that format is not seen as being appropriate for either the higher or the lower strata of workers. While the review system within an organisation should be standard, it is crucial to allow scope for different types of review at different levels within the organisation.

- It is not making best use of the review system to give everyone within the organisation, irrespective of position and rank, the same kind of interview and the same final report.

Reviewing lower levels of staff

A common reason for not reviewing lower levels of staff has to do with organisational philosophy, the artificial barriers often created between 'worker' and 'manager'. The workers lower down the hierarchy are seen as less valuable and as having less potential than those with higher rank, and it may be hard for them to get promotion. This attitude is changing now, at least in some industries, but unfortunately there are still many organisations that function in this way.

Failure to review the lower strata of workers can lead to a waste of resources. At first sight, review of workers who carry out generally routine activities may seem a waste of money, especially when performance can be judged very easily (number of letters typed, number of machine bits drilled) and without a review interview. So why bother reviewing this section of staff? One reason is to ensure you are not ignoring potential within these groups. Performance review provides workers with the opportunity to suggest ideas that might benefit the organisation, and to give themselves a sense of responsibility and 'belongingness'.

Discovering potential
The worker on the assembly line who has potential for promotion will find it difficult to prove this to the organisation. For one thing, assembly lines function at a particular speed, so the operative often will not even be able to show above average performance on any objective production criterion. The job is designed to be so routine there is no scope for flexibility, so the individual will not be able to display initiative in other ways. Without a well-designed review system, that can in some way (not necessarily just through interviewing but also using techniques such as group exercises) demonstrate who has leadership potential, the operative who has potential will remain trapped in the wrong job. He or she may become frustrated, decrease overall productivity and leave, all because the organisation didn't provide a suitable appraisal system.

Reviewing higher levels of staff

A reason often given for not reviewing the higher levels of staff is that it is hard to find someone senior enough to do the review interview. It is also harder to establish performance criteria. Many people in such positions refuse to accept performance review, perhaps declaring that their position proves their worth to the company, and if the company doesn't accept that evidence then they will think of moving on. If this situation arises, performance review may not be the best approach! But, even for high-ranking executives, performance review can provide benefits. A review carried out by the personnel director on the managing director can be justified in terms of authority. Even though the personel director may be lower in 'rank', he has authority as head of personnel.

It is becoming more common to review professional staff such as teachers, doctors, scientists, etc. Difficulties that are particular to reviewing some of these groups are considered later in the book (see page 131).

Reviewing older staff

Another group that can be left out of the review process is older workers. It is often assumed that someone who has passed 50 (or even worse, 40 or 30!) has peaked and is too old to be considered for transfer, promotion or training. This is a wrong assumption. In the modern world there are ever greater numbers of people who are changing jobs and organisations more often and later in life. It is no longer the norm to stay with the same organisation throughout one's working life. A 50-year-old person may still have 15 years of work left before he or she retires, possibly more. To be able to make use of their knowledge and experience, and perhaps adapt them to new roles, may be very beneficial to the organisation. But the organisation cannot assess whether that person is suitable for retraining or transfer unless he or she is reviewed.

People represent a financial investment, and that investment is not always fully utilised. Performance review, at all levels, is a way of ensuring that the investment in human resources is more efficiently used.

KNOWING HOW AND WHEN YOU SHOULD REVIEW

How to review

There are a number of stages to consider regarding the structure of the performance review, the review itself, and the follow up:

1. Both you and the reviewee should be trained in appropriate techniques, e.g. **interviewing, negotiation, counselling skills**. It is crucial that you both have the appropriate skills, so that you can interact on a similar level in the interview.
2. You should decide why the review is to be carried out. For example: to **set performance objectives, assign rewards/ punishments, determine training needs, promotion, transfer, selection, redundancy, vocational guidance, future potential, job redesign**, or a combination of some of these factors in the form of a regular review.
3. You decide what **data** to collect for the review, e.g. **performance criteria, supervisor ratings**, and consider how the data can be collected.
4. You talk to the reviewee to discuss the forthcoming review and its purposes, and to let the reviewee make suggestions as to content. Any changes to the purposes of the review can then be made.
5. The data are collected. They should be relevant, objective and unbiased. The data can take the form of a **discussion document**.

6. When the data have been collected, they are summarised in a **report** made available to both you and the reviewee. The information should be understandable to both parties. Any complex analyses should be fully explained.
7. The reviewee is given time to digest the report and come up with **discussion points** arising from it.
8. Design the interview carefully, planning it so that all relevant points can be discussed. These can arise from assessing the reviewee's previous objectives and success at attaining them, from the report, from discussion points the reviewee wishes to raise, and from negotiation, where the two parties agree on the reviewee's future **objectives**.
9. The review can now take place.
10. **Performance review report**. This can be written up by yourself or by the reviewee, and should include information on points discussed, conclusions reached and objectives set. It should be signed by both parties to say that they agree with the content. There will also be space for the other party to add comments. This report ensures that no one can later dispute the agreements reached.
11. **Follow up**. It is important that whatever was promised in the review is actually provided. This is the purpose of a review system, e.g. if you promised a certain type of training, then that training should be given.

When to review

When there are reviews for measuring performance against objectives, perhaps based on training, they must be carried out regularly, at least annually and, if appropriate and practical, more often. In this way continuity of assessment is ensured. An effective review can be a good motivator to a good employee, so it is worth doing regularly. There doesn't *have* to be a reason for the review apart from a simple check on performance objectives: have they been reached? If not, why not? What new objectives should be set?

There are good reasons for reviewing individuals at other times. These include:

• after being in a new post for a short period
• if a promotion becomes available
• after a probationary period for new employees

- after promotion or transfer
- when introducing new responsibilities
- after disciplinary procedures.

Nevertheless it is important not to have a series of interviews; work should be disrupted as little as possible. Reviewers should ensure that all relevant aspects are covered at the regular performance review.

ETHICAL CONSIDERATIONS

Performance review raises questions of fairness, openness, equality and trust. **Fairness** relates to the way different reviewees are treated. **Openness** refers to allowing both yourself and the reviewee access to all information that is going to be used in the review (though this may not always be possible). **Equality** refers to the equality of yourself and the reviewee as to your respective roles in the interview itself, rather than your status within the organisation. **Trust** refers to the confidentiality that must be respected in the dialogue.

Fairness

All individuals within the organisation should be treated in a similar fashion when they are being reviewed. This does not mean that they must all receive the same type of review, but it does mean that the same guidelines are used for designing the review, carrying it out, and reaching conclusions and judgements about performance. If the data used in the review are objective, and collected properly, and the review itself is well planned, then the outcome is more likely to be fair. This subject is discussed in more detail later.

Openness

In order to carry out an effective review, both parties – you, representing the organisation, and the reviewee – must as far as possible be fully knowledgeable about all the information that is to be used in the review. Openness leads to honesty and trust, and openness on the part of the organisation will encourage the reviewee to express themselves fully, without fearing that the organisation is hiding information.

On the whole, openness within the review can be achieved.

There are many organisations, however, which would disagree with that. Perhaps they think it best not to let the staff know the organisational objectives, or the overall sales figures for the previous year. Why is this? Why do they keep information from staff? Staff should be encouraged to be part of the organisation. If they know what is happening, if they know the present performance and future plans of the organisation, they are more likely to feel part of that organisation. They will then be motivated to work more effectively, and have much more job satisfaction.

Openness benefits both sides, bringing more profit for the organisation and more satisfaction for the individual.

A survey has shown that 92 per cent of reviewees see some of their performance review report, but part of the report is often still secret. There is a largely unfounded fear among managers that total openness would lead to blander, more lenient reports. Research has shown, though, that where reports are open, managers are just more *careful* about what they write, rather than less frank. They are more likely to obtain evidence for their position.

Equality
A sense of equality between the reviewer and the reviewee is important. The reviewer will usually be senior to the reviewee, but that doesn't mean a sense of equality can't be engendered. Both parties need to be able to talk freely, to exchange ideas without fear of rebuke.

The lower-ranking reviewee
The usual situation is that you as the reviewer are of higher rank than the reviewee, and this can make it difficult for the reviewee to speak openly, especially when wishing to criticise the organisation. (This is particularly difficult if you are the reviewee's supervisor. It is suggested later that, for this reason, the reviewer should not always be the immediate supervisor or line manager.) In these cases it is crucial that any implied threat about speaking one's mind is removed.

The higher-ranking reviewee
The other problem of equality is one alluded to earlier, that of the reviewee being of higher rank than yourself. This problem may be

eased by using personnel staff as the reviewer, though the review still remains a potentially threatening situation.

The element of threat can be removed if both you and reviewee understand the reasons behind the performance review, its purposes and the way it operates. You are then both more likely to accept your roles within the system, and to act appropriately. It is important that reviewees are shown *why* they should be on equal terms with you. If they see the benefits they will act appropriately.

-isms
One of the main dangers facing a performance review is whether sexist, racist or ageist attitudes and behaviours are present. Many such attitudes and behaviours, though not overtly expressed, still make reviewees feel threatened. The reviewer must take great care here – not only is sexism etc. morally wrong, there are also legal implications to consider.

Trust
Confidentiality is essential in performance reviews. If reviewees don't believe they can trust you to act confidentially regarding whatever is discussed in the interview, then they are less likely to say what they think. For example, there may be a delicate under-lying personal problem. If the reviewee can share this with you appropriate action can be taken, but if they don't trust you then nothing will get done and the problem will remain, and may become more serious over time.

PSYCHOLOGICAL TESTING, COUNSELLING AND NEGOTIATION

Psychological testing
Most performance reviews make no use of psychological testing. This is unfortunate because, in certain circumstances, testing can provide much useful information very quickly, particularly with the advent of computer-based tests. There are many different tests that measure many different areas of human performance. The most important ones are **aptitude** and **ability tests** that help assess whether an individual has the right kind of abilities to do particular jobs, and **personality** tests that will demonstrate strong and weak characteristics and help build effective teams. Tests are particularly useful when the review is for promotion or transfer, as

they are good predictors of performance in new situations. (See Chapter 4.)

Counselling skills

It is crucial that you have basic counselling skills, so that you can cope properly with personal issues and problems that emerge from the review. A reviewee handled badly in this situation can be expensive, both in human and financial terms. (See Chapter 3.)

Negotiation

Basic negotiation skills are needed by both parties so that in cases of disagreement it will be easier to work out solutions to problems. Without such skills, when neither party can effectively argue their case, the review may revert to dominant/subordinate roles with you imposing your will on the reviewee, for example when setting objectives for future performance. By using negotiation skills it is more likely that an arrangement fair to both parties will be arrived at. (See Chapter 3.)

CASE STUDY

John ignores ethical issues

John Parkin is a middle manager in a medium-sized company in the south east. His responsibilities include selection and performance review within his department. Though he has many years of managerial experience, is popular with most of the workforce and is expected to rise further in the company, John operates an implicit sexist policy. The only ones who know about this 'policy' are John's colleagues in his department and, partly perhaps because they are male, they do not consider it an issue worth protesting about.

Put quite simply, John will not employ females in the workshop, as supervisors, or as managers. He will only employ them in clerical roles. This policy is not questioned by the company because: one, they do not operate any checking system on the categories of people employed, and two, the type of work carried out by John's department has always tended to be a male-dominated area.

John considers his performance review system to be very efficient. There is no company-wide policy, responsibility being delegated to departmental heads. John reviews everyone regularly, he gives them adequate time for preparation, has an excellent interview technique, covers all the right issues relating to both the organisation and the reviewee and invariably follows up with appropriate action. Unfortunately, the same system doesn't apply to female members of the clerical staff. For this group, John's first (and to him most important) question is: 'When are you going to get pregnant?'

Comment
This example illustrates how an apparently good performance review system is rendered invalid by a single individual operating a policy that is unknown to the company (and in this case illegal). The situation would be improved by the company:

(a) adopting a company-wide performance review system that involved systematically training reviewees and ensuring they treat everyone fairly by collecting appropriate data, and
(b) because it is a tradionally male-dominated area, having a positive discrimination policy to encourage females to enter the company and to ensure that once there they are treated fairly.

OUTLINING THE REST OF THE BOOK

The following chapters go through the stages of designing a review, running it and following up.

- Chapter 2 considers purposes of performance reviews.

- Chapter 3 is concerned with how individuals should be trained to perform optimally in the performance review.

- Chapters 4, 5 and 6 cover the actual preparation for the review interview, from deciding who should carry it out, to determining the purposes of the review, collecting and summarising relevant data, allowing both parties to suggest discussion points arising from the data, and structuring the interview.

- Chapter 7 considers the review interview: when and where it should be held, the interview itself, and the report.

- Chapter 8 considers following up the performance review with specific actions, and assesses the effectiveness of the performance review system itself.

- Chapter 9 draws a number of conclusions.

All case studies in this book broadly reflect real life experience, though all the individuals are entirely fictional.

SUMMARY

This chapter has shown how performance review:

- Involves effective communication between the individual and the organisation. It encompasses a broad range of situations.

- Is often poorly designed, over- or under-ambitious, and in-adequately resourced.

- Should be objective and unbiased, and take into account the needs of both the individual and the organisation.

- Is necessary for all workers, from directors of large organisations to shop floor workers.

- Should be well structured throughout from training the participants properly, setting objectives, preparing for the interview, the interview itself, to follow up and validation.

- Should be carried out regularly, at least annually.

- Should be fair and open, and promote equality and trust between the participants.

EXERCISES

1. How might different individuals or groups be treated unfairly in an performance review?

2. Consider the way you conduct reviews at work. List the areas where your technique is (a) good, (b) may need improving. Include anything to do with the way you prepare for the interview, how you conduct the interview, and how you act on the outcome of the interview.

3. How would you go about reviewing a senior director in your organisation?

2

Knowing What Performance Review is For

This chapter will consider the purposes of performance review in terms of:

- Defining the purposes well in advance of the interview.

- Minimising conflict between the purposes of the review as the employer and the employee see it.

- Maximising performance for the organisation.

- Maximising job satisfaction for the individual.

- The specific purposes of the review.

BEING CLEAR ABOUT THE PURPOSE

A major problem with performance reviews is when the participants do not know what they are for. Often their purpose is not clearly defined. They consist simply of an interview between an individual (the reviewee) and his or her immediate supervisor (you, the reviewer). These interviews may have some structure, or just be general chats about the reviewee's performance. They may be based on little or no objective data about the reviewee, and as such have little real value.

Another problem seems to lie in an apparent conflict between the purposes of the performance reviews as the organisation sees them, and the purposes as the appraisee sees them. This conflict is largely imaginary, but it is reinforced and perpetuated by the behaviour of both the organisation and the reviewee. As the reviewer, you may be keeping much of the data obtained for and from the performance reviews secret, and the reviewee may believe the organisation is trying to catch them out and find an excuse for not giving them a full bonus, or not promoting them or, in the worst case, dismissing them.

This chapter describes the main purposes of performance reviews. Anyone trying to set up a review system should, before doing anything else, clarify the purposes of the appraisal. This determines everything that follows, from the selection of appropriate data to designing the interview, and the conclusions to be drawn from it.

Types of review

Never lose sight of the fundamental reasons for all reviews:

* to maximise job satisfaction for the individual

* to maximise performance for the organisation.

Remember, in a good review system these are not conflicting reasons; they are complementary.

Most reviews are carried out with a limited number of purposes in mind. It is not usually helpful or necessary to design a single system that incorporates all or even most of the following general purposes. For example, a review to assess the performance of an individual new to the organisation will consider the performance of the individual to date. It will look at training needs that have emerged in the first few months, and perhaps consider future potential, possibly providing some guidance on how the career of the individual could progress over the next few years. The regular performance review would not necessarily consider training needs on every occasion, nor would it make use of psychological tests. Thus different types of reviews cover different areas.

CONDUCTING THE REGULAR PERFORMANCE REVIEW

The performance review is extremely important, as it helps to build up a picture of the performance of the organisation, and of its individual employees. It is crucial to carry out this kind of review regularly. It is often done annually, but it could be carried out every six months, or even every three months in certain circumstances. This depends on:

* the philosophy of the organisation regarding human resource management

* the individuals involved in the review performance

- the content of the review
- the cost of the review (in time and money)
- the general economic situation as it affects the organisation.

It is important that the procedure remains largely similar year upon year (apart from necessary updating of the system). This will help in making direct comparisons of performance over several years. Some authors have argued against this, on the grounds that if an individual had one particularly good year, then performance in the future shouldn't be blighted in contrast – or vice versa.

> **By making comparisons the organisation can address why individuals who in the past have done well might be doing less well.**

A pattern may emerge over several reviews. Perhaps there is a gradual falling off in performance, suggesting decreasing job satisfaction, caused by boredom with doing the same job for too long. These comparisons are made possible by keeping all the performance data over a number of years.

Regular performance review systems, if not constantly monitored and upgraded, may become obsolete in time. This is why validation needs to be constantly carried out to check whether it is doing its job (see Chapter 8). It is a key element of any review system. It is one of the best ways of checking whether the system is working.

Increasing confidence

The regular performance review has advantages in that reviewees gradually become familiar with what it entails. They become more confident at expressing themselves and more willing to accept performance objectives because they themselves will be part of the decision-making process. This process can be extended, so that the review enables them to make comments about how the organisation as a whole is functioning – a kind of elaborate 'suggestion box'.

SETTING OBJECTIVES

This is the traditional purpose of performance reviews. The reviewee's performance is assessed against previous objectives and, by mutual consent, new objectives are set for the coming year. The objectives must be agreed by both parties. The reviewer has to ensure that realistic objectives, in management terms, are set, and the reviewee must be fully committed to the objectives in order to perform effectively.

Setting realistic objectives

Setting objectives is an important function. It concerns what the reviewee will be doing in the future. The setting of objectives should be a careful process that takes into account a number of factors, including:

- performance against previous objectives

- aptitude at job

- personal circumstances

- future potential

- the changing work environment.

Reasonable objectives give employees sensible guidelines against which to work for the coming year. If these guidelines aren't present, or aren't sufficiently clear, they may not know what is expected from them.

Once you are in the performance review interview, you must be in a position to discuss the objectives to be set for the coming year. All organisations have a hierarchy of objectives, from corporate to employee. Here we need only consider the employee's objectives. What should they reasonably be expected to achieve and, very importantly, what **performance criteria** should be used?

Performance criteria

These should be chosen carefully, especially for situations where performance is not easily quantifiable (e.g. management). There is little point in setting objectives that aren't measurable in terms of actual performance. For some jobs, quantifiable assessment is easy, for others it is more difficult. But for any assessment of performance the criteria chosen should be rational, allow systematic measurement, and be stable over time. Stability enables the organisation to monitor individual and organisational trends. Possible criteria include:

- direct financial indices, such as sales volume or profit
- direct quantitative measures, such as units of production or number of customers
- ratios, such as errors per 100 transactions or sales per 100 contacts
- time factors, such as time it takes to complete a task, or ability to meet deadlines
- judgemental scales, such as supervisor ratings, peer ratings, and ratings of inferiors
- open-ended questions
- descriptive opinion.

These can be categorised into quantitative or qualitative criteria (with a gradual decrease in quantitativity as one reads down the list). Quantitative data is usually easier to obtain and analyse, but care still needs to be taken to ensure extraneous factors have been accounted for. For instance, if the criterion is 'sales volume' then account should be taken of size of sales territory, number of potential customers, number of actual customers, time spent in the field, experience, and any other factors that might have a bearing on the criterion.

Qualitative data may appear to be more vague and subjective, but in the end they can offer much richer sources of information, as long as they are collected with care – as long as the right questions are asked.

It is often useful to use quantitative data as a starting point, and to expand on these with qualitative data.

Appropriate interpretation of qualitative data is also critical. Such interpretations may be inevitably subjective, but it should not be unfairly biased.

Objectives and organisational structure

Objectives depend on the organisational structure. Does the organisation set individual targets at a level above the reviewer? If so you will not be able to use your negotiating skills very much because you won't have the authority to set targets. In extreme cases, you will simply have to tell the reviewee what must be achieved in the coming twelve months. Cases like this don't help create effective reviews, or lead to good employee relations. Indeed, they should not really be considered as reviews at all, because they involve little or no interaction between the organisation and the individual, and will not serve the crucial purpose of ensuring employee job satisfaction. There is little point in having a performance review if it is only to instruct. The employee might as well be sent a letter! The point of the review is to enable *discussion* to take place.

You need to know the upper and lower limits of your negotiating position, and to encourage the appraisee to accept higher objectives – but only if this is feasible based on evidence regarding past performance, and other matters that arise out of the review procedure.

Performance-related pay (PRP)

The review system can be used to determine levels of PRP where this is applicable, though there are inherent dangers in any such system, particularly regarding fairness. If PRP does not apply across all employees then it is likely that those outside the system are going to resent those who are in it and the organisation. While this issue is somewhat outside the remit of this book, it is highly recommended that any PRP system applies to all employees – or none. A system applying to some subsection will be seen as unfair by others, particularly if the level of PRP for, say, a manager, is affected by the performance of employees who are not in the system. Any organisation applying such an unfair system is in danger of alienating employees outside the system.

Your power to give praise, recognition and criticism

The reviewer is in a useful position to apply praise, recognition and criticism. We are all familiar with the benefits of praise, of recognising a job well done, which in turn leads to a sense that the employee feels that the organisation is recognising them as an individual. It is important that you take advantage of the situation to provide appropriate praise.

Criticism is also important. If an individual's performance has been poor for some reason, it is perfectly acceptable to criticise, but it is important that this criticism is constructive. If it isn't then criticism can be demotivating, which will only exacerbate the problem.

> **Criticism has to be supported by constructive comments about how to improve performance.**

DETERMINING TRAINING NEEDS

Employees should have access to any training courses that will help their performance and career development. The review interview can help determine training needs in a number of ways. You can:

- ask the reviewee
- ask the reviewee's supervisor
- assess flaws in performance and discuss how these might be rectified
- apply appropriate psychological tests
- look into the reviewee's record to see which courses have already been attended.

There is little advantage in sending employees on training courses without accurately assessing their particular needs. Individuals and jobs differ so much that off-the-peg training courses are likely to be wasteful of resources.

Instead of meting out criticism if the reviewee isn't performing effectively, the performance review might bring out that the real reason is that the reviewee doesn't have the necessary skills. To give a simple example, the reviewee might have been given the job of negotiator for buying certain goods. In other buying functions they may have performed well, but faced with trained and experienced negotiators they are out of their depth. Without analysing the situation, you may decide to punish the reviewee in some way (e.g. withhold a bonus); but if you carry out the assessment properly, you will find that the reviewee simply needs training in basic negotiating skills.

Determining training needs
Training needs can be determined in a number of ways. These will depend on the particular need, the person involved and the situation itself (organisational objectives and climate, availability of particular training courses, etc.).

Asking the reviewee is useful because they are the ones who often know their job best, and can to some extent judge their own effectiveness and where their weaknesses lie. These weaknesses can often be offset by training.

The supervisor of the reviewee is also a good person to determine training needs.

Other issues may arise from the performance review itself, or from the data collected for the interview. For instance, a personality questionnaire may have established that the reviewee lacks assertiveness, yet is in a role where assertiveness is a positive characteristic. If this result is discussed in the interview, and the reviewee agrees with the result of the questionnaire, then you can recommend the reviewee to go on an assertiveness course.

ASSESSING OTHER PURPOSES OF PERFORMANCE REVIEW

Promotion and transfer

Promotion and transfer are separate but linked purposes of performance reviews. They are separate in that promotion involves moving to a higher status post while transfer doesn't (and may indeed involve a demotion). The link is that both involve the reviewee moving from one post to another.

This type of performance review involves more than an assessment of current performance and prediction of future performance in the same post, i.e. the basic performance review procedure. Here judgements are made about the individual's potential to do well in a *different* role. Of course, that role may be very similar, in which case past performance may be very relevant; but where the roles are very different, the reviewer should be very careful about making judgements as to which candidate will perform best in this new role. It is unwise to assume that just because someone is doing exceptionally well at their present job they will do equally well in a new role. The new role may well involve very different job tasks and perhaps much more responsibility.

The danger of promoting someone too high, to their level of incompetence, is sometimes called the 'Peter Principle'. If this occurs, neither the organisation nor the individual will benefit. It is likely that the organisation will lose money by having an incompetent person in a particular position, and the individual will be dissatisfied trying to do a job for which they are not well suited.

The role of psychological tests

This is where psychological tests can help. Tests are useful for helping make predictions about future performance that are not based on past performance (at least, not in the same way as a simple review is). Measuring the characteristics of people already performing that new role, and finding out what it is that separates the better performers from the weaker ones, allows the reviewer to establish a template against which to measure those individuals who may be transferred or promoted to that role – though final decisions should never be based solely on test scores. (For more details on psychological testing, see Chapter 6.)

Performance review as selection interview

When considering promotion or transfer, the performance review takes on the role of a selection interview. The design of the interview should be altered accordingly. This is described in detail later. The review may still consider previous objectives and performance, but it may not be useful to discuss *future* objectives. This is because it is still undecided who will be promoted. While it is necessary to discuss the general performance requirements of the job, there is little point in discussing particular objectives with someone who is not in that particular role. It is a waste of resources, as specific objectives set will partly depend on the person appointed. Thus a promotion review should not be part of the regular performance review. It should be quite separate.

Selection

Selection is not usually seen as a form of review, and perhaps the boundaries of the concept are being stretched a little. However, review systems are part of the overall human resource management of the organisation, and so is selection. The selection process is similar in structure and content to the promotion/transfer review, except that in selection the 'reviewees' are outside the organisation. In fact there is greater overlap than this, because applicants for a particular post often come from inside as well as outside the organisation. This is the main justification for including selection reviews here.

If there are applicants from both within and outside the organisation, it is fair and efficient to subject both groups to more or less the same procedure. This will include an interview that is well-structured, and based on certain types of data, such as:

- the application form, which reveals details of skills and interests (often as a CV)

- references or supervisor ratings (depending on whether the candidate is external or internal), which give an indication of past performance (references should be obtained on a form similar to that completed for supervisor ratings)

- psychological tests which are, when used correctly, the best predictors of future performance.

There will be differences in the way internal and external candidates are treated, simply because the organisation usually knows more about the internal candidate. These differences shouldn't adversely affect the selection procedure, as both types of candidate will in the end be assessed on the same person specification.

Redundancy

Strictly speaking, this is not a form of review at all. If employers use the term 'performance review' for determining redundancy decisions, they undermine the value of the performance review system, since for employees the threat of the sack will be associated with all performance reviews, irrespective of what they are told.

Redundancy reviews are carried out when the organisation, for whatever reason, has to cut back on its staff. It makes economic sense to make the least well-performing individuals redundant. These reviews are therefore designed to assess performance (rather than optimise job satisfaction), to find out who is performing at a standard below that required, or who is doing relatively worse than other employees in similar positions. If there is little to distinguish between performance, then length of service is usually the next factor taken into account, with the general rule that those who arrive last leave first.

In this type of review it is crucial that you display counselling skills (see Chapter 3), and build vocational guidance into the procedure.

Redundancy is not always the only answer to an overstaffed department. It may be possible to transfer the individual elsewhere.

Vocational guidance

Guidance should be provided where the individual is made redundant, whether compulsorily or voluntarily. (Terms like 'outplacement' are still sometimes used, but they are euphemisms I choose not to apply to what is a very difficult position for the people involved.) It is fair to do so, as the situation is not brought about through any major fault in the employee, apart from in some cases having a relatively poorer performance record than other employees. There is even more reason for the organisation to help if the employee has been made redundant after long service.

This again moves slightly away from the usual definitions of performance review, but it is linked. Some say that vocational guidance isn't and shouldn't be part of performance review. But we began by saying that performance review means ensuring the right person is in the right job, maximising both job satisfaction and productivity. If the organisation is dismissing the employee when that employee hasn't committed a misdemeanour, then the organisation is morally obliged to do all it can to help that employee find another job in which he or she will obtain maximum job satisfaction.

Vocational guidance techniques
The most effective vocational guidance involves the employee completing a series of questionnaires and psychological tests. These will provide a great deal of information about the individual, including aptitudes, personality and interests. The right psychological tests will generate ideas for the right kinds of careers. A structured interview can be designed to explain these findings to the employee, and suggest the types of jobs that may be suitable, and how to go about obtaining further details.

The organisation should also ensure the redundant worker has all the necessary skills for obtaining another job, such as:

- writing a curriculum vitae (CV)
- filling in application forms
- interview techniques.

By providing this service, the organisation goes some way to ensuring the leaving employee has a reasonable chance of obtaining a new job that will prove satisfying.

Assessing future potential

Assessing future potential is not the same as a review for promotion or transfer, where there is a specific vacancy available and the organisation is looking for someone to fill it. Here the purpose is to find out which employees are likely to rise through the ranks. It is also used to identify who might be suitable not necessarily for promotion, but for transfer to a different department, perhaps to do a quite different job.

High-flyers

It is important to find out who is likely to be a 'high-flyer' so that they can be prepared for their future roles, which will probably involve a great deal of training. If a person seems suitable for higher management, then they can perhaps be placed on a programme of courses designed to prepare them for that kind of role. Accurate assessment is crucial in these cases because training is usually very expensive; if the wrong individual is chosen the organisation may waste a lot of money.

Transfers

Likewise, if someone looks as if they may be more suited to a different type of job within the organisation, perhaps a transfer to a different department, they should be prepared for that. This may again involve training, or perhaps a temporary transfer to see how they get on.

What data are needed?

In order to assess future potential, you will need various types of data. Past performance is not necessarily a guarantee of future performance in a different role, but that doesn't mean it is of no value. It is useful to introduce ideas from selection, even though here there is no specific job for which the reviewee is being selected.

It is helpful to question the people the employee works with, to interview colleagues, supervisors and subordinates. It is important to create a general picture of the work the employee carries out, the problem inherent in the job, etc., and to carry out a similar process for the job to which they may be transferred. Psychometric tests are used by many organisations to obtain information about people. Such tests are useful for ascertaining general abilities and specific aptitudes, to find out how individuals might perform in a different setting.

> **It is important that test results should be interpreted with care. They do not provide solutions, they provide clues to solutions.**

Using these findings as a basis for discussion, the review can draw out further information to complete the picture, and to determine the best direction for the employee's career. This type of review also decreases the risk of possible future job dissatisfaction. For instance, if the reviewee is not using their aptitudes to the full in their present post, then dissatisfaction is likely in the long term unless there are promotion prospects to take them to their level of ability. The personal profile of characteristics obtained from the reviewee can also help identify training needs. If the reviewee shows a flair for a certain subject, brought out by an aptitude test, then this flair can be trained and brought into use in the organisation.

Job redesign

Performance reviews are useful to help discover how jobs themselves, rather than the individuals doing them, are at fault. This is a review of the *job* rather than the *person*, so again the boundaries of the concept are stretched.

Jobs are often badly structured or inappropriate. Many jobs in a lot of organisations are simply a hotch-potch of tasks, thrown together to serve a particular purpose at a certain time and built up in a relatively random manner over the years by different people taking on various tasks at different times. If the personnel department tried to analyse this kind of job they would typically fail to find any coherence. There would be no reason why these miscellaneous tasks should be put together to be carried out by one person under a single job title.

When the organisation has jobs like this, it is useful to carry out a review of staff to determine their views on how the job might be designed in a more coherent way. The organisation might find that an apparently hotch-potch job is being done by a person who is perfectly happy doing that particular range of tasks, in which case it may be more efficient to leave the job as it is. Or they may find that the person doing it is immensely dissatisfied, in which case a radical job redesign may be necessary. In both cases, the importance of the review is that it allows the organisation to assess the views of staff.

A review carried out to assess the need for job redesign is more of an advice and information gathering session than one designed to assess the reviewee. Yet it still falls under the general heading of performance review because it is concerned with contact between organisation and reviewee to increase productivity and job satisfaction.

Review related to job redesign is only needed rarely, and in organisations that have for some reason become inefficient because of the incoherent nature of the jobs its employees are doing. Individual job redesign reviews may also be needed when particular employees are unhappy with the pattern of tasks they are required to do, and the appraiser will need to see whether the tasks can be redistributed in a better way. In this case much preparation for the appraisal interview is needed, to see what the options are.

INTEGRATING OBJECTIVES

These various purposes of performance reviews are often closely linked within a single interview. They are not designed to exclude each other. Interviews should rightly concern more than one of the above categories. For instance, if you are carrying out the regular performance review, you are likely to include an assessment of training needs, future potential, and the setting of objectives. It is more cost-effective to put them together as a single package, as usually happens in practice, rather than have two or three different interviews that upset the flow of everyday work and don't really achieve anything extra.

That doesn't mean that *all* the above have to be included in every regular performance review. *Each* appraisal interview should be carefully designed, and its purposes clearly laid out, even when relatively informed. Reviews carried out between times largely concern particular job openings (promotion and transfer).

ADDRESSING PROBLEM AREAS

Many managers feel that the handing out of praise and criticism should be kept separate from the rest of the performance review, particularly when it may include criticisms by the employee of the organisation or of the supervisor. If rewards are assigned separately, so the argument goes, the employee can be more open with the reviewer, and develop a better sense of trust. If the reviewee thinks you are forming subjective judgements on the basis of these criticisms (for example as to whether or not a full bonus is deserved!), and that you have the power to withhold bonuses, then trust can be hard to establish and the reviewee will not state their viewpoints openly.

This problem is difficult to resolve. In some cases it may be possible to set up objective criteria for the award of bonuses. In others it is not. If objective (and fair) criteria are available, then there is no reason why rewards should not be linked to the review system. If not, then they *cannot* because the reviewee would not jeopardise the chance of obtaining a bonus by, for example, criticising the way the organisation is run if the reviewer was the boss!

Even the best review systems are, like anything involving humans, open to abuse. For example, the reviewer may try to set objectives that the reviewee believes are too high, or the data used in the interview may be perceived as inaccurate or biased. A good review system gets around this problem by having **grievance procedures** and **arbitration** where reviewees can approach other authorities if they believe they have been treated unfairly.

CASE STUDY

Jack finds a better strategy

Robert Oldfield is being appraised by Jack Coupland, and has already covered various aspects of his performance over the last six months when Jack says:

'I'd like to turn to this problem you're having with stock levels. I hear that levels are so low you're having difficulty meeting orders on time, and that the Whitesons order was two days late. You need to make sure levels are adequate. You can't afford to be late with these orders.'

'Yes, but the problem is . . .'

Jack interupts: 'I don't want to hear why, I just want it sorted out – quickly.'

Clearly, there are a lot of problems with this interchange. A better approach might be:

Jack: I'd like to turn to this problem we're having with stock levels. I've been told by despatch that we're having difficulty meeting orders on time, and one order was late. Can you tell me about it?'

Robert: 'Yes, it's true I'm afraid. Stock levels had been kept down because we had been having problems with high levels. If you remember we discussed this a few months ago and agreed to decrease levels. Now, we have all these extra orders production are having difficulty keeping up.'

Jack: 'Yes, I see what you mean. What do you think we should do about it?'

Robert: 'Well, we're over the worst of it now, stock levels are rising again, and I think we can get the orders out on schedule. But for the future, if we had more information from marketing I don't think the problem would have arisen. We just weren't prepared for the extra orders.'

Jack: 'OK, I'll get on to marketing and make sure you get the information you need. I suppose monthly would be all right?'

Robert: 'Yes.'

Jack: 'What about future stock levels?'

Robert: 'If I get the right information from marketing then we can keep them down to our previously agreed figure.'

Jack: 'Right, we'll give it a try.'

Comment

You can see the difference between the two strategies. In the first Robert isn't given a chance to put across his position. He is simply blamed for what had gone wrong and told to put it right. This strategy may well lead to resentment and hostility. The second dialogue is much better. Here, Jack draws the information out of Robert by asking open questions, 'Can you tell me about it?' and then asks Robert for his own solution: 'What do you think we should do about it?' The problem is presented, the solution is found, and appropriate action is planned.

Also, Jack uses 'you' in the first dialogue. This isolates Robert from the company, suggests the problem is entirely his and that he alone has to find the solution. In the second dialogue 'you' becomes 'we', the problem becomes a company problem, and the company will work together with Robert to find the solution. The use of 'we' in this context is less likely to alienate the reviewee and thus less likely to create resentment against the organisation.

SUMMARY

This chapter has shown how:

- The purposes of the performance review should be clearly defined well before the interview takes place.

- There is no real conflict between the purposes of the review as the employee sees it and as the organisation sees it.

- Effective reviews should maximise performance for the organisation.

- Effective reviews should maximise job satisfaction for the individual.

- Performance reviews are used for a variety of purposes.

EXERCISES

1. Look at the list of purposes for carrying out reviews given above. Which ones are used in your organisation? Give reasons why the others aren't used.
2. List three benefits of review for (a) your organisation, (b) yourself.
3. What kinds of data are used in your organisation for performance reviews? Are they objective or subjective?

3

Acquiring the Necessary Skills

This chapter will consider the appraisal skills required for:

- Both parties, such as interviewing techniques, negotiation and listening skills.

- The reviewer, such as job analysis, basic conselling skills and designing the interview.

- The employee, such as preparing for the interview and developing self-awareness.

A review system cannot work properly without due regard to the training both you and the reviewee need in your respective roles. There are a range of skills both parties need to carry out the review properly.

One problem that can arise is to get managers to admit to their weaknesses regarding the skills required. They may believe they have the requisite skills, such as interviewing and negotiation, when this is not the case. It is the responsibility of the organisation to ensure the appropriate skills are acquired.

One cannot separate the different skills required by individuals involved in reviews; they are too closely linked. For instance, those listed below under the heading of 'negotiation' largely apply to general interviews. These skills are considered separately for the sake of clarity.

INTERVIEWING SKILLS

There are many kinds of interviewing situation and they require different kinds of skills, such as:

- selection interviewing (both one-to-one and panel)

- media interviewing

- performance review interviewing.

Certain rules apply across all kinds of interviewing, including the review interview. Interviewing is a **communication skill**. Before an effective interview can take place, both parties need to know what the other party expects. If both parties agree on the *purpose* of the interview, it is more likely to succeed. If not, then neither party will really be listening to what the other has to say. Since they are expecting different things, they will hear different things. Suppose you are only interested in reviewing the performance of a reviewee and setting new objectives for the coming year, but they wish to discuss training needs. You may find yourselves talking at cross-purposes and achieve little except mutual dissatisfaction. You will realise that the reviewee is dissatisfied, and they will be unhappy that their training needs haven't been met. This shows the need for each party to *listen* to what the other is saying.

Empathising

A good interviewer or interviewee will always try to appreciate the other person's point of view, to try and understand *why* they are saying what they are saying, as well as *what* they are saying. This leads to **empathy**, and an increased likelihood of mutual goodwill. It is then more probable that conclusions can be reached which are satisfactory to both parties. In the example above, if you listen to the reviewee's views on training, and act on them, the outcome of the review is more likely to satisfy both parties.

The purposes of the interview

These may be:

- to establish training needs
- to assess past performance and provide appropriate praise/criticism
- to set targets for future performance
- to determine suitability for promotion/transfer
- to assess future potential.

Within the general framework, each party may wish to raise specific points. For example, the reviewee may wish to complain about poor supervision. It is useful if the reviewer knows that this point will be raised in order to prepare an answer to it. This is rather like Question Time in the House of Commons, where the questioner presents the question well in advance, so that the minister has time to formulate a well-considered answer.

Finding background information

If you know the reviewee has a problem with supervision before the interview takes place, you can look into the possible reasons behind it. In the interview itself you are only going to hear the reviwee's side of the argument, and it would be extremely unwise to base any decisions on partial data. Before the interview takes place, go and see the reviewee's supervisor and get their view. The supervisor may not realise there is a problem, and a chat with the reviewer may itself solve it. Perhaps the supervisor is unaware of some personal circumstance of the reviewee that is affecting work performance, such as overtiredness due to a new baby. If the supervisor thought the poor performance was due to laziness then it is likely that this would cause trouble between supervisor and reviewee. In this case the solution is simple: the supervisor should be more sympathetic with the reviewee, and perhaps transfer some of their workload temporarily to ease the situation.

This example is an illustration of a lack of communication, the major cause of organisational inefficiency and employee dissatisfaction. The review system is designed to increase communication.

In many cases the solution won't be this simple. For instance, if there is a personality clash between the supervisor and the employee, it may only be soluble by transferring one party (usually the employee). The important point is that it is *crucial* that you make an effort to understand both sides of any problem, before the interview.

Preparing for the interview

It should not be necessary to say that both parties need to be prepared for the review interview, but in many real life cases one or both parties go into the interview not knowing what they are going to say, or how they are going to respond to what the other party is going to say. This almost guarantees an unsatisfactory outcome.

Both parties should be prepared

Once the purposes of the interview have been established, the way to obtain a better outcome is for *both parties* to work out what information they need to collect for the interview. They should prepare answers to questions the other party is posing, and prepare their own questions. More attention is paid to the collecting of information in the next chapter, because this is a key issue in performance review. Relevant information should be collected and collated, and a copy of the **pre-review report** given to both you and the reviewee before the interview. From this simple document both parties can prepare questions and discussion points.

Both parties in the appraisal need to be aware of the **structure** of the interview. The design of this will usually lie with you, as the one who first determined the purposes of the review. You will now decide *what* should be discussed and *when*, ensuring a part of the interview is open for the reviewee to raise issues they consider important. Thus the structure of the interview is controlled by you. This does not harm the interests of the reviewee, as long as they are given a chance to raise the points they feel are important. The structure of the interview will be considered in more depth later.

NEGOTIATING SKILLS

It is important for both you and the reviewee to have good negotiating skills. Negotiation is not a process whereby two parties start from different positions and reach a compromise that satisfies neither party.

- The aim of good negotiation is a **win-win situation** where, even if both parties start from a different standpoint, they can both feel they have benefited.

Getting a sense of equality

One important prerequisite for good negotiation is a sense of **equality** between the two parties. This may be a particular problem in the relationships between men and women. You may be of higher status than the reviewee, and it may be difficult to achieve true equality. If the two parties need to negotiate away their differences, then the reviewee must not have to fear any recriminations for acting without regard to your usual status.

It may be difficult to attain true equality between individuals of different status. Unconscious processes can come into play. Reviewees may not put forward propositions and ideas as strongly as they should, and may also be more ready to accept ideas that you propose. The opposite may be true for you, as you may put forward ideas more forcefully, and be less likely to listen properly to the ideas of the reviewee. This illustrates the importance of both parties *consciously* behaving as equals. This will minimise the problem.

Eight rules for successful negotiation

There are certain **rules** that should be followed in order to negotiate successfully. Some of these may appear a little harsh, particularly when trying to design an interview that is open and fair, with both parties interacting on a friendly basis. Many of the rules of negotiation don't seem conducive to such behaviour, but remember that they are based on strategies used by skilled negotiators bargaining between organisations. They are not necessarily harsh; it depends on how and where they are used. The review interview is very different from negotiating at an organisational level, but the same rules apply to both situations.

If both parties are aware of the rules, of the way each other is behaving, misunderstandings are less likely to occur.

The rules are:

1. Avoiding irritators

These include words and phrases that have little positive effect on the negotiation, but irritate the other side. This might include suggesting that your own position is 'fair' when it patently is not, or implying that the other party's position is not fair. This category also includes offensive and insulting statements, or statements based on incomplete information: for example, if you tell the appraisee that they are 'incompetent' because they haven't achieved certain targets, without looking into the reasons why the targets haven't been met.

2. Avoiding counter-proposals

Here, one side makes a suggestion, and the other side makes a counter-suggestion, totally ignoring the suggestion from the first side. This is an issue of listening. As mentioned elsewhere, listening is important in any review interview. If one party ignores the other by simply presenting its own position, it is not listening. For instance, the reviewee may say 'I have not achieved my productivity targets because the reports have not been reaching me on time.' The reviewee is suggesting that there is a communication problem within the organisation. Instead of agreeing to look into the matter, you may simply suggest that the targets haven't been reached because the reviewee does not manage time effectively, and so you recommend a time management course. In other words you have not listened.

3. Avoiding aggressive behaviour
Beware of allowing the interview to get heated, when conflict and hostility become overt. The situation can quickly spiral out of control, though it is unlikely to occur in many interviews for a number of reasons. Even though a sense of equality may be present, the reviewee may be a little afraid of displaying too much equality, such as acting aggressively towards you. Likewise you may well feel that acting aggressively may be exploiting your own superior status in a way that is unacceptable You are also in a position to ensure disagreements do not become open conflict. Knowing each other can either increase or decrease the risk of aggressive behaviour. If there is personal animosity between the reviewer and the reviewee there may be problems in the interview. It is your responsibility as reviewer to ensure the interview does not become unprofessional.

4. Avoiding argument dilution
'Argument dilution' occurs when one person justifies a position by using too many supporting arguments. This is a self-defeating process as the more arguments one uses in support of a position, the more likely it is that the other party can effectively argue against that position, by turning one of these supporting arguments around. Once one argument collapses, the whole position may collapse.

For instance, the reviewee may argue that they need a particular type of training, using a whole string of arguments to support their position, such as increased productivity, benefits outweighing costs, efficiency, increased knowledge base, and the future potential of the individual. The organisation may not be able to argue against most of these reasons, but may not believe the reviewee is likely to stay long enough to justify the increased outlay. So the final argument, future potential, can be used by you to justify not expending resources on training the reviewee. Thus the reviewee, instead of providing a list of solid reasons why the training should be provided, has undermined their own position by presenting too many reasons.

5. Behaviour labelling

This is a technique used to keep the discussion rational, and to slow it down. It involves tagging statements with **prior indicators** that show what the individual is going to say. For instance, instead of saying, 'I would like a pay rise' the reviewee might say 'I'm going to ask you a question. I would like a pay rise.' This technique can be used when the discussion seems to be losing direction, or when issues are being covered too rapidly. Behaviour labelling enables either party to slow the discussion down or get it back on course. It is a simple but effective technique.

6. Testing understanding and summarising

This is used to ensure that the party has understood what the other party is trying to say, and to give themselves time to think of a response. If you have made a proposal, and the reviewee wishes to make it clear in their head, it is useful if they repeat it in their own words and check with you to ensure it is understood properly.

For example, if the discussion has centred on training needs, you should sum up by stating in simple terms the agreed training needs of the reviewee. For example, 'It seems then that you would benefit from a course on report writing, which should improve the quality of your writing and ensure reports reach your supervisor on time. Would you agree with that?' If you have made an error, this will immediately become obvious when the reviewee responds, 'I do agree, but you have not mentioned my need for training in stress management that I mentioned earlier.'

7. Seeking information

Suppose the other party has put forward a proposal, but has not fully explained their position. The good negotiator will ask for the further information required. This is also a useful strategy for controlling the situation. A carefully directed question will steer the discussion in a particular direction. 'I know you are unhappy in the sales department, but you say you have a talent for marketing. Would you explain to me why you believe you would be more suited to the marketing department?'

8. Feelings commentary

This phrase describes the way individuals express their feelings. Effective negotiators are more likely to express the way they feel than ineffective negotiators. In the case of performance reviews, if you express your feelings – and are perhaps openly critical of some aspect of the organisation – you are more likely to obtain the trust of the reviewee. It shows you are willing to let your guard down, to 'expose your throat', and the reviewee is then more likely to state their position more openly. This of course is also an important aspect of counselling.

Understanding the data

In the next chapter, various forms of data are described that can be used in the performance review. Some of these are fairly complex, and so both parties may need training in order to understand them. For instance, if a personality questionnaire is administered to the reviewee, to understand the results both you and the reviewee need to appreciate the definitions of the traits that are used, and the explanations for the results put forward by the psychologist. If supervisor ratings are used, it is important that all parties (reviewer, reviewee, supervisor) interpret each rating in the same way, otherwise understanding, and hence communication, will be adversely affected. If one question reads, 'Rate the reviewee on overall performance', apart from being a badly worded question which the supervisor probably won't understand, it may be interpreted in different ways by each person.

Active listening skills

It is important for both parties to engage in **active listening**. This is crucial for a good interview. They should show each other that they are being listened to properly, not simply heard, by concentrating on what is being said and not losing interest. The basic rules are:

- don't make hasty judgements
- don't listen selectively
- don't interrupt
- feed back the information to ensure it has been heard properly.

The reviewer who makes hasty judgements without hearing all sides of an argument is ineffective. If you don't listen to all the reviewee has to say then you may miss something of value. Likewise for the reviewer who listens selectively. If you have decided before the interview what your conclusions will be, and only hear what you want to hear, then why have the review at all?

Apart from being simple rudeness, constant interruptions can upset the flow of the reviewee's comments. Interruptions are justified when the reviewee (or the reviewer for that matter) is rambling, or when one party doesn't understand what the other is saying, but not otherwise. If something comes to mind, then instead of interrupting, make a note of it, to enable you to remember what to say once the speaker has finished.

GAINING REVIEWER SKILLS

You may well need training in job analysis, interviewing techniques as an interviewer, basic counselling skills, and on how to design performance review interviews. There are also a number of other skills required that are harder to categorise, but are listed below.

Job analysis

A key element of interviewing is the job analysis. If there is no adequate job description available, this analysis may need to be carried out before the appraisal. This is described in more detail in Chapter 5. It will suffice to state here that by analysing the job of the reviewee you learn about that job in very great detail. You become aware of:

- how the job is carried out

- the objectives that are reasonable to set someone performing the job

- the limitations on performance imposed by the job

- how the job might need to be changed

- the role of the job within the organisation.

You won't always have to go through the whole process of job analysis and job description. In more efficient organisations, up-to-date and complete job descriptions will be on hand, but the good reviewer should not always rely on this information being available. There is no point in using a job description that is out of date (and they can become out of date very quickly). The information may be wrong. The best way to find out whether a job description is out of date is to ask the person performing the job, and perhaps their supervisor.

Interviewer skills

Interviewing involves more than an informal chat between two people, or a set of questions chosen simply because they 'sound good'. Accurate conclusions cannot be drawn from this kind of situation. A good interview needs to fulfil certain requirements, including:

- the right location

- creating a relaxed atmosphere

- asking the right questions

- structuring the interview (are the questions predetermined or do they arise from the interview itself?)

- personal skills

- recording the data accurately.

These requirements will ensure that as much useful information is extracted as possible.

You need to learn the right interviewing skills for standard performance review purposes, and also for staff selection purposes, if you are involved in that.

Question-formatting

Certain interviewing skills are specific to the role of reviewer. **Formatting the questions** themselves is an important one. Questions should normally be open-ended, that is, force the reviewee to answer in greater detail than in a simple yes/no fashion. For example, 'why do you think your performance has been below standard recently?' is better than 'Has your performance been below standard recently?' The former leads to a better two-way discussion. You can respond to the reviewee's answers with further questions to explore the information obtained; ideas expressed can be linked together better, and clarity will be ensured. It is inefficient to go on asking closed questions, and leading questions such as 'Your performance has been poor because your husband left you, hasn't it?', though closed questions can be useful for gathering basic information.

Counselling skills you will need

It is important for you to have basic counselling skills, though you should never try to take the place of the professional counsellor. There are plenty of experts, should that be necessary. The reason for you having training in counselling skills is that these skills are likely to be needed at unpredictable times. For instance, when the reviewee is discussing the reasons for poor recent performance, they may blurt out that their partner is about to leave them. This situation calls for a little tact and diplomacy on your part.

You basically need to be gentle, to display empathy with the reviewee, and display good listening skills. Counselling is not a matter of telling someone what to do. It is essential for the individual to make his or her own decisions. The most that the counsellor can do is to offer advice – if appropriate.

Counselling skills are also important in the redundancy appraisal. If the reviewee knows the potential consequences of a poor performance, it can be quite traumatic. In cases where the reviewee knows he or she has been sacked, the situation is equally serious in a vocational assessment appraisal, as they may be experiencing personal problems.

Designing the interview

It is essential that the interview is well-structured. This isn't just a matter of ensuring you collect the right information in the interview, though clearly this is the desired aim. In order to achieve this aim you should carefully consider the purposes of the interview, the collection of preliminary data, and the form of the interview itself.

Other important skills

Effective use of data

You need the ability to use available data effectively, to consider various options, and to put these options to the reviewee in a reasonable fashion. This involves a great deal of skill and tact. You could simply set high targets and tell the reviewee to achieve them. It is more difficult, but more effective, to *sell* the options to the reviewee, to show them how the objectives are reasonable. This in turn will lead the reviewee to internalise the objectives, to accept them more fully, and be more willing to act on them.

Thus the reviewer's role is partly one of selling, but selling ideas rather than goods or services.

Constructive criticism

You must criticise in a constructive fashion. It is easy to criticise someone's less than perfect work, but it is harder to criticise without isolating the reviewee and losing their trust. Don't spend the whole interview tearing apart the reviewee's work. That is not constructive. Apart from disillusioning the victim it is also a waste of time. If there is a need to criticise then do so in a reasonable fashion, and follow up with constructive suggestions as to how to improve things. For instance, if a manager is always rushing around trying to organise things without seeming to get anything done, it is right that they should be criticised. But if this is followed up by the constructive proposal that they should attend a time management course, then the criticism becomes productive.

A firm manner

You do need a certain firmness of manner, which should be used at appropriate times. It is for you to keep the interview on course, to keep to the structure of the interview and not allow serious diversions. If the interview is going astray, you should bring it back to the subject in question. Firmness of manner means assertiveness, not aggression. It means ensuring you keep control of the situation, always politely, but always with authority.

Discretion

It is essential that you are discreet. The reviewee must be able to trust you to keep whatever is discussed confidential. They will be more open if they trust you not to reveal anything you have said in confidence to other people.

Objective judgements

You should be able to make objective judgements based on accurate data in an unbiased fashion. This is not necessarily easy, especially if you are the reviewee's supervisor and there is antagonism between you. If there is bad feeling, it may be best if the supervisor is not the reviewer (see Chapter 4).

Supervisor ratings

Another skill you will require, and one often not given due consideration, is the ability to design and use supervisor rating forms. This involves:

- designing supervisor rating questionnaires that are appropriate to particular circumstances
- training supervisors etc. to fill them in correctly
- interpreting them accurately.

Supervisor ratings (Chapter 6) are often used as performance indicators. Use them with great caution as ratings are necessarily subjective judgements.

GAINING EMPLOYEE SKILLS

The skills required by the reviewee were largely covered earlier, but there are a few points to make. The reviewee is the interviewee, and like any interviewee wants to come out of the review 'looking good'. In order for this to happen they must:

- be prepared
- put themselves across well.

The reviewee is in a different role to the selection interviewee, as they usually know you, and 'first impressions' will not be a relevant consideration.

Preparing for the review

Reviewees should assess their performance over the period under consideration. It is important for them to relate performance to previously set objectives, so that when you ask questions useful answers can be provided. It is also important to try to ensure that as many as possible of your questions are anticipated, and answers prepared.

Preparation should also be made regarding the future. What sort of objectives ought to be set? What training is needed? In what direction is the reviewee's career going? Is the level of responsibility adequate? How should performance be improved? Treat the review as a career evaluation. It is a chance to try and change things that are wrong, to improve one's conditions and circumstances, and create opportunities for career development.

Developing self-awareness

Reviewees should analyse their own strengths and weaknesses before the interview. This skill is called developing self-awareness, and involves the ability to congratulate or criticise oneself appropriately. It is harder to acquire than might be imagined. The reviewee has to consider the areas where he or she was particularly successful or unsuccessful, and look into the reasons why.

CASE STUDY

Philippa's employers fail to communicate

Philippa Harvey was regional sales manager in the south west for Proctor's, a large firm of paper manufacturers. She was very happy, she was very good at her job and everyone knew it. Her region consistently outperformed other regions, and this was in large part due to her personal efforts. Then Philippa was told unofficially by her friend, Rachel Jones at Head Office, that the vacancy for the post of national sales director was going to become vacant soon, and that she was by far the best candidate – if she was interested. She was very interested, and when the post was publicised she applied immediately.

That was when things began to go wrong. When she heard nothing for a few weeks, she telephoned Rachel to find out what was happening. Rachel was very evasive, and said that the directors hadn't considered the applications yet. So Philippa waited another couple of weeks. Finally, she received a letter which said that unfortunately she had not got the post, but thank you for applying.

Philippa was livid. She repeatedly phoned Head Office for an explanation but got nowhere. She felt rejected by the organisation, and this showed in her work, which deteriorated quite considerably. After a couple of months, during which time she was far from happy, she was called to Head Office for performance review. The reviewer was Ashley Edwards, one of the directors.

The interview was very heated. Ashley knew that Philippa had been turned down for the Head Office post in favour of someone from outside the organisation who was very experienced at this level. What he wasn't prepared for was the level of Philippa's anger. When he told Philippa why she hadn't got the post she just managed to control her temper and explained that she felt the company had let her down very badly, that after so many year's experience they had not even interviewed her for the post – though she was supposedly the best candidate – and they had not discussed with her the reasons why she hadn't got the post. Anyway, who was this person who had got the job? As the company was only interested in talking to her now when they saw weaknesses in her performance it was obvious they still didn't care about her needs. At that point she resigned.

Comment
Philippa was obviously very valuable to the company; she had attained the status of regional sales manager and was performing very well. They didn't want to lose her. When the national vacancy arose it is unfortunate that they didn't even interview her, to show they appreciated her talents enough to consider her for the post. The breaking-point came when her rejection simply consisted of a short non-explanatory letter. Instead of this letter Philippa should have been told face to face that she hadn't been given the post, and the reasons for the decision explained (i.e. a kind of performance review). It is important for organisations in this situation to show they value the individual. Proctor's did not do this and so they lost a good worker.

SUMMARY

This chapter has considered:

- Training in interviewing techniques, negotiation, understanding and interpreting data, and listening to the other person.

- Training for the reviewer in job analysis, basic counselling skills and designing the interview.

- Training for the employee to prepare for the interview and develop self-awareness.

EXERCISES

1. Think about the training you have had for carrying out reviews. Does it cover all aspects of the reviews you carry out? In what areas do you need further training?

2. A member of your team is due for a performance review. What are the main issues that should be addressed when preparing for the interview?

3. How should you train someone in negotiating skills?

4

Understanding the Role of Reviewer

BEING PREPARED

This chapter will consider the role of the reviewer:

- For example line manager, supervisor, employer, human resources manager.

- There are arguments for and against each of these. The final choice will depend on the organisation and the employee.

Preparation is *crucial* to the success of any performance review. Both you and the reviewee need to put a lot of time and effort into preparing for the review, or it will not succeed.

Several decisions have to be made before preparations can begin for the review interview. You, representing the organisation, usually decide:

- when the interview will occur

- what its purposes are

- the data that need to be collected

- the structure of the interview.

This chapter, and the two following, consider the decisions being made when preparing for the review. These include:

- who should be the reviewer

- the purposes of the review

- the type and extent of data to be collected

- how the data should be collected

- preparing the pre-review report

- ensuring the appraisee has seen and understood the report

- determining discussion points arising from the report and any other sources

- ensuring each party understands what the other wants to achieve

- planning the interview itself.

WHO SHOULD DO THE REVIEWING?

There are various candidates for the role of reviewer. They include:

- the line manager

- the reviewee's immediate supervisor

- the employer

- the personnel manager

- a specially trained appraisal officer whose major function is to carry out staff appraisals.

There are valid arguments for all these individuals to be the reviewer, and equally valid arguments why none of them are ideal in all circumstances. The choice of reviewer will depend on such factors as availability, type of review, rank of the person being reviewed, and size of organisation. Small organisations may not have individuals who fill all the roles above. Few organisations, even large ones, have anyone whose major function is to carry out reviews, as in the past the role of reviewer has been part of the function of the line manager.

Assessing the arguments for and against each of these?

The immediate supervisor or line manager
This is not always the best person to act as reviewer, though in most organisations they do. Admittedly there are good reasons *for* the appraisal being carried out by such a person. Others may know too little about the reviewee's work, or the general work of the department, particularly if it is very specialist, such as a design department. They may be unable to assess previous performance accurately or to provide reasonable objectives. These problems can usually be surmounted by a reviewer with some knowledge of what the reviewee does, by carrying out detailed research into the

job before the interview, and ensuring adequate data is available about both the job and the person.

The best argument *against* the supervisor or line manager carrying out the review is their close working relationship. In certain circumstances this may make it difficult for either or both parties to express themselves fully, especially if the reviewee wishes to criticise the standard of supervision. The reviewer and reviewee have to work together on a daily basis, so any antagonism between them might reduce productivity and job satisfaction for both.

Furthermore, the supervisor, because of the closeness of the relationship, may not be in the best position to assess the reviewee's work.

Sometimes, a reviewee's poor performance may be caused by difficulties in their relationship with their supervisor. For example what if the supervisor doesn't respect the abilities of the reviewee, or is always criticising their work? When reviewees are questioned about their poor performance their answer is unlikely to be honest or complete. How do you tell someone you are not working very well because you don't like the way they treat you? This review may end without the two individuals getting to the root of the problem, which will then persist and may indeed worsen.

> **The reviewee needs to be able to talk to someone freely, to someone distanced from the situation, about whatever problems they feel exist.**

There is another problem with using the supervisor or line manager. To do reviews effectively, reviewers need training, as we saw in the previous chapter. If the organisation has to train all its supervisors and line managers to do this, costs may become unrealistically high. Far better to train a small group of individuals very well than many individuals poorly.

Using the employer
The best argument *for* the employer carrying out the performance reviews is that they will, by assessing the performance of all employees, learn a great deal about how the company functions. A cynic might claim that this is also the best argument *against* the employer carrying out the reviews!

In reality, the employer is the best person to carry out reviews in small firms, but the time factor is clearly going to militate against this in bigger firms. Reviewing staff takes time. An essential component of smooth operation it may be, but the employer has many roles to fulfil. Nevertheless reviewing staff is likely to be an efficient use of time, as it enables the employer to develop an understanding of the needs of employees.

The use of the employer as reviewer may, in larger organisations, involve too large a difference between the status of reviewer and reviewee. It may be difficult to establish a sense of equality at the review interview. There is also the problem that the employer may not know enough about particular jobs and their requirements.

Using the human resources manager

The human resources manager's job is to ensure that the human resources of the organisation are functioning properly. This may mean anything from employing the right numbers of people in the right jobs to making sure pay packets are filled correctly at the end of the week. Performance review interviewing clearly falls within the role of the human resources manager and this is the best argument that they should carry out the interviews. They will be conversant with the review system, with the jobs, and with the people doing the jobs. In medium-sized firms the personnel manager may be able to carry out some reviews. In larger firms, the human resources manager has overall responsibility for the review, but the reviews themselves should be done by other members of the personnel department.

Using the specially trained performance review officer

In larger organisations reviews should be carried out by in-house specialists. There are a number of reasons for this:

- A specialist reviewer will have detailed knowledge about the jobs carried out within the organisation (by reading job descriptions, interviewing employees, etc.).

- A specialist will appreciate the philosophy and objectives of the organisation, yet be able to interpret these in terms of individual employee needs.

- A specialist will be trained in the various skills required for effective reviews.

- A specialist will be able to analyse the results of reviews across the organisation and advise what targets to set, which departments are performing best, where problems lie, etc.

- Finally, perhaps most importantly, the judgements a specialist reviewer makes will apply in a similar fashion *across the organisation.*

On this last point, if the reviewer assesses individuals across the whole organisation, they will be able to make objective, comparable, and thus fair judgements between employees. Consistency between individuals is particularly important, especially when the purpose of the review is promotion, transfer, redundancy, praise/criticism or determining training needs.

So who should be the reviewer?
There can be no single answer to this question. It depends mainly on:

- the size of the organisation

- the purposes of the review.

Generally speaking, though:

- If the organisation is very small (i.e. where the employer has not separated the role of personnel from other functions), the employer is the right person to carry out the review.

- In medium-sized firms the human resources manager is the most appropriate appraiser.

- In larger firms the specialist reviewer in the personnel department will be able to carry out most reviews most efficiently.

The line manager or supervisor is *not* appropriate if it is likely to damage the personal relationship between reviewer and reviewee after the interview, or if the reviewee is not going to speak out for fear of the consequences. In favour of using line managers, they are the ones who are most likely to know the reviewee best, to know the job best, and to know the problems that have occurred or might arise in the future. If the line manager is used it is essential that there is a system in place for the reviewee to have the opportunity to discuss in confidence with another individual any problems they might have with the line manager.

The use of line managers and supervisors as reviewers depends largely on the personality of the individuals and their day-to-day relationships with the employees. Organisations need to base their decisions on a systematic analysis of their own circumstances, resources and needs.

Selection reviews
If the review is for promotion/transfer or selection, it would be appropriate for the appraiser to be a manager from the department having the vacancy rather than a specialist from the personnel department. The organisation is examining the candidates for a vacancy and trying to place the right individual in it. The manager from the appropriate department will usually be more aware of the needs of that department than someone outside.

Specialist reviews
If the reviewee is a specialist, such as a research scientist, it may be inappropriate for a reviewer to come from outside the department. It would be unreasonable to expect that reviewer to know enough about the work of the scientist. After all, the training of a scientist takes many years and it would not be possible to condense it all into a short job description! In such cases the reviewer needs to be someone from the same department, with similar specialist knowledge. But even here care is needed. The review may, if not carefully prepared, become too cosy, with the needs of the organisation coming second to the needs of the scientists within the department.

- This illustrates the need to be conscious at all times of the purposes of the appraisal in terms of the needs of the particular *organisation* as well as the individual and the department.

KEEPING THE OBJECTIVES IN VIEW
The purposes of performance review were discussed in detail in Chapter 2. In summary, they are:

- regular performance review
- setting objectives
- determining training needs

- promotion/transfer
- selection
- redundancy
- vocational guidance
- assessing future potential
- job redesign.

As noted earlier, these objectives are not mutually exclusive; several may be covered in the same interview.

It is crucial that the purposes of the review are determined and understood right from the start. If you don't know exactly why the review is being carried out, how can you possibly begin to organise it? If the reviewee doesn't know why they are being appraised, how can they formulate arguments and discussion points?

By being aware of why the review is being carried out you will know what to include in it. If it is for a regular performance review, it will probably include setting future objectives and assigning PRP. Other elements will be included as and when required. The reviewee may wish to include purposes such as determining training needs. If the reviewee has just finished a probationary period, the review will probably include an assessment of future potential. Reviews for promotion/transfer and selection arise out of organisational need.

Apart from the regular performance review (which should be standardised across employees), reviews arise out of **need**, either the need of the organisation or the need of the individual employee.

For details of these types of appraisal, see Chapter 2.

CASE STUDY

Jacqueline gets the wrong reviewer

Graham Sanders is a manager at Cloggs Shoes, a footwear manufacturer. He supervises the sales staff. He is also responsible for reviewing the sales staff. Graham is very unpopular because of his rather authoritarian approach. He supervises by ordering people to do things, never considering the viewpoint of his subordinates. If the task is done well he rarely praises, if it is done badly he frequently criticises. All sales staff have an annual performance review, along with more frequent meetings to discuss particular issues that arise.

Jacqueline Horner was very nervous about her interview. She did not like Graham, and on top of that, she had problems at home that were affecting her performance at work. Her poor performance was regularly criticised by Graham, who had little sympathy for personal problems. He strictly separated home life from work life, and expected everyone else to do the same. This criticism affected Jacqueline's performance even more.

When the interview started, Graham got straight to the point: 'Your performance has been deteriorating for the last six months, and it can't go on. You have to do something about it or you're out.' Jacqueline really needed to discuss why her performance was suffering, but she couldn't talk to Graham. She had little to say in response to Graham's charge, and the interview ended with even more hostility and dislike than there had been before it. After the interview Jacqueline went straight to see Graham's superior, to discuss what had happened and to find some way to sort out her problems, one of which was now her supervisor.

Comment

Jacqueline should have been reviewed by someone other than her supervisor because part of her problem became the supervisor. Though the main problem was her personal difficulties, these were exacerbated by Graham. She needed to talk to someone who would be sympathetic, about both her personal difficulties and the quality of her supervision. If her supervisor had been more empathetic regarding her personal difficulties then maybe they wouldn't have affected her work performance.

Situations like these, where the employee is forced to 'go behind the supervisor's back' to a third person, can lead to further problems, ones that wouldn't have arisen had the original review been carried out by someone other than Graham.

SUMMARY

In this chapter we saw how:

- There are various possibilities for who takes on the role of reviewer: line manager, supervisor, employer, personnel manager/officer, specially trained review officer.

- There are arguments for and against each of these being the reviewer. The final choice will depend on the organisation and the individual being appraised.

EXERCISES

1. Who in your own organisation is most likely to carry out reviews? List reasons why this is (a) a good idea, (b) a bad idea.

2. Think of the members of your own team. What is the optimum time (or year, month, week, day) for them to have their regular performance review? What are your reasons for this?

3. Are there cases in your own organisation where a specially trained performance review officer would be (a) more effective, (b) less effective, than a line manager for carrying out reviews?

5

Devising Job Description and Person Specification

This chapter will consider the importance of understanding the job and the person:

- Ideally, data should be objective and unbiased.

- The job description should be up-to-date and complete.

- The person specification should be clear.

DECIDING WHAT DATA ARE NEEDED

Several types of data are relevant to performance reviews. You need to decide which are necessary *after* you have determined the purposes of the review. Data should not be collected for the sake of it. There is little point in using psychometric test results for an annual review. Similarly, all data that are relevant should be collected. If you haven't obtained supervisor ratings and comments, and the reviewee suggests that they are not getting along well with their colleagues, you will not be able to form a balanced judgement about why these problems exist. The reviewee may suggest that the problem lies with colleagues, but the supervisor may suggest that the problem lies with the reviewee. You need both sides of the argument.

While it is desirable that data are objective, it is rarely possible. Subjective data in the form of interviews and discussions are the norm in many types of performance review, and this should not be problematic. If the participants are aware of the potential pitfalls of subjective or qualitative data (bias against individuals and groups, reliability, etc.) then the system can be fair and unbiased. Errors of judgement always arise because the participants are people, but they should be minimised. Procedures need to be in place to ensure fairness and validity (see Chapter 8).

The major types of data used are:

- job description
- person specification
- performance criteria
- previous objectives
- psychometric testing.

The first two relate specifically to the needs of the job, and are considered in this chapter. The others relate to the individual reviewee, or the interaction between the reviewee and the job, and are considered in the next chapter.

CREATING A JOB DESCRIPTION

This is an essential type of information, particularly where you are not fully conversant with the job. As mentioned earlier, the job description should be *up-to-date* and *complete*, otherwise you will not be certain of the nature of the reviewee's job. In efficient organisations up-to-date job descriptions are available, but unfortunately this is not often the case. If there isn't one, you will have to devise one. The more you know about the reviewee's job in the first place, the easier it is to devise a job description.

The process of formulating a job description can be very time-consuming, and you may need help to do it. If the appraisal system is going to succeed, the help of the personnel department in ensuring job descriptions are up-to-date is essential. A specialist reviewer won't have the time to devise these job descriptions.

What follows is a simple method of devising a job description. The description should be revised regularly using the same process. Jobs can change in character over quite short periods of time, partly because of the individuals involved in the job, who share tasks, transfer tasks, etc., and partly because of the organisation which may change the tasks involved. Many of these changes are peripheral, but it is important to incorporate them in the up-to-date job description. They may, for example, affect the personality requirements of the person carrying out the job (and hence the person specification for it).

Devising the job description

The first step is to carry out a **task analysis**. Basically this involves analysing the job to identify:

- what tasks are done
- how long they take
- how often they are carried out.

There are various ways of obtaining this information:

- Check whether an old job description exists. If there isn't a detailed one there may be a summary that has been used for advertising purposes.

- Observe the job being done, though this is very time- consuming, and may not be practical for many jobs.

- Ask the reviewee to keep a diary of the tasks carried out over a particular period of time, perhaps a few weeks. You can then analyse these tasks in terms of frequency, time taken, etc.

- Interview the reviewee to see whether any preliminary conclusions you have drawn are valid. The reviewee is a useful source of information about the work. Other tasks they do may not have been included, in which case these and others can be discussed in more detail.

- Interview others doing the same job.

- Interview the supervisor.

- The personnel department may be able to help reveal aspects of the job that are neglected, i.e. not carried out by the reviewee.

- There are various published questionnaire methods of job analysis, such as the Saville & Holdsworth Work Profiling System, which is a computer-based questionnaire to be completed by the worker; this focuses on tasks, contexts and personal attributes, and can also be used to generate person specifications. There is also the Positive Analysis Questionnaire, which is an older American system consisting of 187 items relating to the job and the work environment which cluster into six areas concerning the job structure: information input, mental processes, work output, relationships, job context, and other characteristics. If you are going to use such sophisticated tools, it may be wise to employ a psychologist to ensure the questionnaires are used effectively.

In order to identify the key elements of the job, where the reviewee's abilities are being put to the best use, ask the supervisor to record **critical incidents**. He or she is asked to recall incidents that showed someone doing the job in an excellent manner, and others that showed them doing it badly. These incidents will show which elements of the job are crucial and also help devise the person specification, described in the next section.

Figure 1 is a sample form for the **task analysis**, followed by explanatory notes for filling it in.

Putting the job description together

The information that you have built up using the task analysis can be put together into a job description. The job description contains five areas:

1. *Purpose of the job*: sets out the organisational objectives of the appointment.
2. *Position in the organisation*: shows to whom the individual should report, his or her department, perhaps including an organisational chart.
3. *Principal duties and responsibilities*: lists the key tasks the individual will perform. It also indicates level of authority.
4. *Specific tasks*: sets out in more detail what particular tasks have to be done and how they are carried out.
5. *Working relationships*: refers to those with whom the individual has contact, whether superiors, subordinates, colleagues, or people outside the organisation such as customers, salespeople.

The job description also includes information about the personal factors required of an individual doing the job and the education and training needed.

The job description is used in the performance review interview as the major yardstick against which to assess performance. A job description is needed for all types of review. An example of a job description form is given in Figure 2.

TASK ANALYSIS

Job title   Department:

Company: Date:

Reviewee's name:

Supervisor's name:

Reviewer's name:

Task	Knowledge/Skills	Aptitudes	Personality
1.			
2.			
3.			
4.			
5.			
6.			
7.			
8.			
9.			
10.			

Fig. 1.   Sample form for task analysis.

Task analysis: explanatory notes

This checklist is used in conjunction with the job description and person specification. It enables the reviewer to analyse the tasks carried out by the reviewee, and the knowledge/ skills, aptitude and personality characteristics required. It is often useful to obtain help filling it in from the people doing the job and the supervisor.

The task analysis is used for designing the job description and person specification. The questionnaire on page 74 is arranged in four columns: task, knowledge/skills, aptitudes, and attitude.

Task

The individual tasks carried out by the reviewee are entered here. If possible, include a percentage figure for each task showing the amount of time spent on it. If this is not done, it may mistakenly be assumed that the employee spends the same time on each task, and the job description may be misleading if this isn't really so.

Knowledge/skills

What knowledge/skills are required for the task? For instance, educational qualifications, knowledge of a geographical area, and skills obtained at work, etc.

Aptitudes

What general abilities are required for the task? For instance, mechanical aptitude, numerical aptitude, verbal reasoning.

Personality

What personality characterisitics are required in order to do the job well? For instance, patience, extroversion, competitiveness.

Make sure that the task analysis is carried out carefully. Very often a job hasn't previously been analysed in any depth, so the exercise may take a little time, but it will be worthwhile.

JOB DESCRIPTION

Job title: Department:

Company: Date:

Prepared by: Position:

Responsible to:
Responsible for:
Number employed on this work:
Position from which candidates for this job might come:
Avenues of promotion/transfer from this position:

Purpose/objects of work:

Main duties/activities:

Forms/equipment:

Contacts:

Discretion:

Checking:

Supervision required:

Supervision given:

Other responsibilities:

Working conditions/conditions of service:

Personal requirements:

Other information:

Please continue on a separate sheet if necessary.

Fig. 2.   Example of a job description form.

Job description: explanatory notes

It is crucial to understand the nature and purposes of the job. In order to define the job, the tasks involved, and the personal characteristics required of the reviewee, the job description is used.

The following notes will help you complete a job description. Make sure the form is filled in accurately, and in detail.

Purposes of work
A summary of why the job exists, or is being created.

Main duties/activities
A list of the main tasks involved in the job, with some indication of the time spent on each. This information can be derived from the task analysis. Where does the work come from and where does it go to?

Forms/equipment
Does the reviewee need to complete or maintain any forms or records? Give examples. Do they need to use any machines or equipment? Illustrate.

Contacts
Indicate the extent, frequency and nature of any contact with other employees, organisations, or members of the public.

Discretion
Does the work entail following written (e.g. manual) or oral (e.g. supervisor) instructions. How far can the reviewee vary the methods of work or the order in which tasks are done?

Checking
Who checks the reviewee's work, how often, and by what method?

Supervision required
On what matters and how often does the reviewee receive instruction from superiors? What matters need to be referred to a superior for approval, or to be dealt with, and how often?

Supervison given
What authority does the reviewee have as to: assigning work, checking work, discipline, dealing with grievances, recommending appointments, salary increases, transfers, promotion, discharges and performance assessment?

Other responsibilities
Use this section for any other responsibilities of the reviewee that haven't been covered in other sections.

Working conditions/conditions of service
What are the conditions/environment under which work is carried out? What facilities are provided? How long does it take to learn the job? What are the rates of pay? Is it an hourly rate or commission-based?

Personal requirements
Education, skills, knowledge, personality.

Other information
This section can be used to include any information thought to be relevant to the job description that is not contained in any other section.

If a job description is already available, with less information than given here, it may well suffice. But do ensure that your own job description covers all the points raised above.

CREATING A PERSON SPECIFICATION

The person specification describes the individual abilities and characteristics needed for the job, based on the job description. They are ones:

- **essential** for good performance

- **desirable** for good performance

- **conflicting** with good performance, i.e. if the person has this particular characteristic then it is likely that they will perform more poorly in the job because of it.

Six main headings

The person specification includes different sorts of information about the individual, categorised into six points. The information obtained on each point *must* be relevant to the job. Irrelevant information is not included, as it may bias any findings or conclusions. In many cases not all points are necessary. The six points are:

1. *Qualifications:* educational background, including vocational training and qualifications.
2. *Intelligence/aptitudes:* the level of general ability, perhaps measured by IQ, numerical or verbal ability, manual dexterity, etc.
3. *Personality:* is the individual who is good at the job likely to be extrovert, emotionally stable, dominant, aggressive?
4. *Interests:* how might the individual spend their free time? What might they want to do in the future? Are these interests primarily intellectual, artistic, social, practical, entrepreneurial? This information can be useful when assessing an individual's future potential.
5. *Motivation:* will the individual be motivated by money, status, praise?
6. *Appearance/circumstances:* this might include information on sex, age, height, build, tidiness of dress, speech. It also includes family factors, such as availability for travel or moving from area to area. For many jobs a lot of this information would be irrelevant and if so should *not* be included.

It is useful when devising the person specification to use a checklist like the one shown in Figure 3. You can then, using the job description already designed, and perhaps with help from the reviewee's supervisor, fill in the checklist.

Examples

Examples of the use of the six points might include:

- *Qualifications:* a teacher would need an appropriate degree. A bricklayer should be time-served. Sales staff may not need particular qualifications, but a general education to GCSE or A level standard.

- *Intelligence/aptitude:* a component assembler in a factory would need manual dexterity. A bank manager would need a reasonable general intelligence and a facility for numbers.

- *Personality:* a salesperson might need to be extrovert, and perhaps insensitive (so they are not affected by rebuttals). A self-employed person needs self-discipline. A diver needs courage.

- *Interests:* a scientist would need to be interested in analysing new ideas. An engineer needs to be interested in mechanical devices.

- *Motivation:* a salesperson is likely to be motivated by the amount of commission that can be earned rather than the quality of the product. Gardeners may be more motivated by the results of their work than money.

- *Appearance/circumstances:* a store manager has to dress appropriately in a suit. Lorry drivers' families need to accept that they will stay away overnight perhaps once or twice a week.

The completed person specification is a real help when analysing the performance of the reviewee. The reviewer matches the qualities of the reviewee as judged from curriculum vitae, psychometric tests, performance, etc. to the person specification, and concentrates on those areas where there is an apparent mismatch. A mismatch *does not* mean that the person is unsuited to the post. It could be rectified by training, or you may find on discussing the issue with the reviewee that the person specification wasn't accurate or complete, and that a different characteristic was just as appropriate. This is particularly true for personality

PERSON SPECIFICATION

Job title: Department:

Company: Date:

Prepared by: Position:

	Essential	Desirable	Conflicting
1. Qualifications			
2 Intelligence/ aptitudes			
3. Personality			
4. Interests			
5. Motivation			
6. Appearance/ circumstances			

Fig. 3. Example of a person specification form.

Person specification: explanatory notes

The person specification comprises a list of characteristcs sought in the ideal applicant for a job. It is based on inferences made from the job description about the personal qualities required.

The checklist will help ensure all the key qualities are included. Its framework is as follows:

Qualifications
Education, vocational qualifications, experience.

Intelligence/aptitudes
General intellectual capacity. Specific aptitudes, e.g. manual dexterity, verbal ability, numerical ability.

Personality
Personal characteristics required both in order to do the job effectively and to work well with colleagues.

Interests
Intellectual, practical, social, artistic.

Motivation
Money, status, personal esteem, friends.

Appearance/circumstances
Personal, family factors (e.g. locality, hours worked).

The information for the person specification is placed under one of the three headings:

- *Essential*: the qualities placed under this heading are considered essential for the proper performance of the job. It is important not to have too many essential qualities or it may be impossible to find anyone who meets the specifications!

- *Desirable*: qualities that would be useful in the applicant, but not essential.

- *Conflicting*: a very useful category as it is often important to indicate characteristics that would make applicants positively unsuitable.

When using the checklist, the reviewer should try to include at least one characteristic under each heading (i.e. a minimum of six, rather than eighteen characteristics), as this will help describe the 'ideal person' more accurately, thought it is not always possible.

charactistics, where people with widely disparate attributes do equally well at the same job.

- You must always allow for your person specification not being complete and comprehensive. People are individuals, with widely varying skills and abilities.

A key management tool

The person specification is a key part of most reviews, where performance is being assessed and future targets set. This is because:

- It will help determine why a reviewee has failed to reach particular targets.
- It will help both parties get to the root of the problem more quickly.
- It is useful when assessing the reviewee's training requirements with regard to the job.

CASE STUDY

Devising the job description

Charles Turner has just been given responsibility for all marketing personnel. Part of his work involves reviewing everyone in the department. Wanting to be thorough, he wishes to update the relevant job descriptions before carrying out any reviews. Unfortunately, his superiors don't see things the same way. If he is going to update all the relevant job descriptions properly then he will need to spend a large amount of time on the task, and enlist the help of others. Unfortunately the company does not like the idea of Charles spending some weeks revising and updating the job descriptions.

This leaves Charles responsible for something he cannot carry out to the best of his ability. Charles must use the information he has (short job descriptions made up for advertising purposes) for carrying out the reviews.

Charles devises a questionnaire that can be sent to all employees. The questionnaire brings together information on task analysis, job description and person specification. Because people are often loath to fill in forms, Charles partially completes them using the informantion he has. Then, when a review is due, he asks the reviewee to complete the questionnaire, to indicate whether the information is correct, and what should be added and what taken away.

Comment
Using this method Charles has obtained a fairly clear idea of the different jobs in the marketing department without taking up too much company time, and without upsetting the employees with a long-winded, time-consuming questionnaire. He can now carry out more effective reviews.

SUMMARY

In this chapter about the next stage of preparation, we have seen that:

- Different types of data are needed.

- The decision as to which data to use depends on the purposes of the appraisal.

- Data should be as objective and unbiased as possible.

- The job description should be up-to-date and complete.

- The person specification is derived from the job description and tells us about the type of individual who should be employed on the job.

EXERCISES

1. Carry out a task analysis of your own job. What can you learn from this?

2. Write out your own job description and person specification in a form suitable for use in a review.

3. How can subjective data be made more objective?

6

Collecting the Right Data

This chapter will consider how to collect appropriate data for the performance review, including:

- Establishing valid appropriate criteria.

- Supervisor ratings (perhaps behaviourally-anchored rating scales.

- Relating objectives to performance.

- The use of psychometric tests.

- Putting together the pre-appraisal report.

- Establishing topics for discussion.

- Following a clear plan.

The data considered in this chapter differ from those considered in the last chapter in that they are concerned with *the person doing the job* rather than with the job itself. That is, they are ways of assessing the person, both in terms of how they perform in the job, and in terms of their personal characteristics.

USING PERFORMANCE CRITERIA

Ideally, performance targets should be set using criteria that are **objective** and **fair**. How far this ideal is attained depends largely on the circumstances of the review. Many types of data are unavoidably subjective and so should be carefully chosen and standardised as far as possible across all employees.

It is crucial to the success of the review to ensure that data are collected in a valid fashion. For sales staff the criteria may seem quite simple, e.g. the number or value of items sold in a given period. This seems objective enough. But it is not likely to be that simple. Other factors need to be taken into account, such as:

- size of sales territory
- number of customers
- number of potential customers
- experience in job
- type of items sold.

These factors should be accounted for and the reviewee assessed in relation to other sales staff. The person who sells the least number of items may in fact be the most effective performer because the territory is new, very small, and the number of potential customers limited. This illustrates the point that one should never form judgements on the basis of incomplete information. Always incorporate **potential confounding factors**, such as size of territory and number of customers.

Data will often seem subjective when really they are objective and valid. A bricklayer can be assessed by the size of wall built, or the quality of the workmanship. The former are clearly objective data. The latter, if used carefully, need not be a subjective judgement as the accuracy of the bricklaying can be measured in terms of size of mortar joint, whether the wall is level or plumb, and so on.

Measuring the performance of managers

Thus we can view many jobs by carefully selecting and organising the data, but it's not always that easy. How do you measure the performance of a manager – by how subordinates are treated? (This could be measured using subordinate ratings.) Or by the number of tasks completed? How do you tell whether the tasks have been done efficiently, and how do you assess the value of each task? These problems might be solved using the job description, or by comparing performance with colleagues. For instance, does it take the reviewee longer to complete a task than colleagues?

Thus for managers there will probably be a combination of objective and subjective performance criteria, the exact mix depending on the tasks involved. In this kind of job there are two very important considerations:

- The process of task analysis, job description and person specification described in the last chapter should be carried out thoroughly. This is an invaluable aid to obtaining the right performance criteria. The criteria will usually emerge during job analysis.

- The criteria that are chosen should accurately discriminate between the performance of efficient and inefficient managers. The reviewer wishes to know which people are performing best and why.

There is no simple answer to the question of how to assess performance in managerial jobs, but the question still needs careful consideration. It is not efficient to introduce subjective judgements (easy to obtain) simply because it is difficult to find more objective data sources.

Supervisor ratings

One criterion commonly used for management (and many other kinds of job) is supervisor ratings. The supervisor is given a questionnaire to complete where the questions relate to the reviewee. The supervisor is asked to rate the performance of the person on a number of factors using a numerical scale.

Ratings can also be obtained from peers and from subordinates where appropriate. The same rules as for the design of supervisor ratings largely apply, and so they are not considered separately here. There are some complications in interpreting these scales. Findings from peer ratings may be either artificially high or artificially low. They may be artificially low because of the effects of rivalry and jealousy, or colleagues may upgrade each other because they don't wish to be seen in a negative light by the interpreter of the scale. These effects may be diminished if the rating scales are anonymous, though on the other hand the problem may be exacerbated. Reasonable results can be obtained when there is a largish group of individuals being tested, who are all assessing each other. The distribution of scores for particular individuals on particular questions will provide useful information. If the distribution is relatively small, i.e. most people have rated an individual with the same score, then that score is more likely to be accurate. Subordinate ratings involve similar problems to supervisor ratings in that any odd effects can be due to personality clashes. Also, subordinates may not want to be seen as criticising their superiors, but this has a lot to do with the culture of the organisation.

Organisations that wish to succeed will accept the need for con-structive criticism.

Criticisms of the technique
Supervisor ratings have been heavily criticised as a performance criterion, but this is largely because of examples when:

- they are badly designed
- they ask the wrong questions
- they have poor scales
- supervisors aren't trained to complete them properly.

These are important points. Fortunately they do not mean that supervisor ratings as such are useless. Properly designed, they can be very effective in all sorts of situations, and the results they produce can be reasonably (though never entirely) objective.

The right questions to ask
The particular questions that are used in the scale depend on:

- the nature of the job
- the person doing that job
- the purposes of the review
- the nature of the supervision
- the amount of detail required from the supervisor.

The questions should be:

- carefully worded
- unambiguous
- not encouraging the supervisor to respond in one particular fashion
- not be so general as to be meaningless (e.g. 'Is X a nice person?').

You may need professional help in developing suitable supervisor rating scales, though this can be an expensive option and may only be viable in larger organisations. The following guidelines, if closely observed, will help you design good rating scales that suit your own organisation.

The rating system
Regarding the scales themselves, a five-point scale is usually most appropriate, e.g.:

Would you consider X gets on well with his/her colleagues?

Gets on very well				Gets on very badly
5	4	3	2	1

Any more than five points and the difference between any two adjacent points becomes virtually meaningless. For instance, what does a difference between eight and nine mean on an eleven-point scale? Very little. It is not easy to make meaningful discriminations on such a scale.

The reviewer has to make sure the supervisor knows how to use the scales properly. Without training, there are big differences in the way people use the scales. On a five-point scale, some people will tend to use the middle of the range 2, 3, 4, never giving scores at the extreme. Others always use the extremes, effectively responding in a yes-no fashion.

- You have to ensure that supervisors all use the scales in a *similar* way, and that they all use the *full range* of scores available.

Behaviourally-anchored rating scales (BARS)
One way to resolve this problem is to use BARS. The major problem with normal rating scales is their lack of definition: what exactly does it mean to score 2 or 4? If judgements are based instead on observable behaviour, these problems are overcome. The scale should contain a clear definition of the trait to be rated, e.g. friendliness. It should also have a description of the behaviours that can be observed at any level on a scale measuring that trait, e.g. 1 = always smiles at and speaks to colleagues and shows consideration to them, 5 = a sullen person, ignores colleagues and doesn't get involved in social activities.

BARS are put together by deciding the key aspects of job performance (from the job description), then developing 'anchors' by asking appropriate individuals to describe a number of critical incidents (see Chapter 5). These are sorted and assigned to each of the key aspects of job performance. Then the incidents are scaled and a rating scale is produced for each of the key aspects of job performance. The major problem with BARS is that they are highly job specific and expensive to produce, but they are more reliable and more valid than normal rating scales.

An example of a supervisor ratings questionnaire is given in Figure 4.

PERFORMANCE AGAINST PREVIOUS OBJECTIVES

Targets set at previous interviews should be included as part of the pre-review report. They should be clearly related to actual performance so both reviewer and reviewee understand the general level of performance, as well as any particular successes and failures, at a glance. Targets are tied to the particular criteria that are used to determine performance. You can easily obtain the previously set objectives by referring to the previous appraisal report.

Assessing targets

Targets for a salesperson might include total number of sales, number of new customers, number of repeat customers, average size of order, proportions of different products sold, plus whatever else is relevant to the organisation. These numerical figures can be put side by side with actual performance, and successes and failures will be easy to see. If the reviewee has failed to meet the target for new customers then the reasons for this can be discussed in the review. Perhaps they were so busy with old customers there wasn't time to establish many new contacts, or few of the people approached wished to buy the goods. Whatever the reason, the areas for discussion are visible at a glance. An example of a form comparing targets with actual performance is given in Figure 5.

Assessing performance

By using this form performance can be assessed at a glance, and areas where there are particular problems, or particularly good performance, can be readily determined. The original targets can be set by looking at the performance of the sales staff as a whole. Size of territory and number of potential customers are constants. If you have the completed form at the review interview, then

SUPERVISOR RATINGS QUESTIONNAIRE

Please complete the following questionnaire with regard to the performance of [Reviewee]. Please ensure you use the rating scale carefully, as you have been trained.

Return the completed questionnaire to: [Reviewer] by: [Date]

How would you describe your relationship with X?

very friendly	1
friendly	2
cordial but with some formality	3
rather strained	4
very difficult	5

Would you say that X fits in well with colleagues?

very well integrated into team	1
reasonably well integrated into team	2
there are sometimes problems between X and colleagues	3
there are major problems between X and colleagues	4

If you responded 3 or 4, please explain why. For instance, does X have problems with particular colleagues, or are there difficulties all round?

Does X generally have good relationships with his/her customers and other contacts outside the organisation?

very good   very poor
 1   2   3   4   5

When X has a problem with work, does he/she approach you or some other appropriate person for help?

never   sometimes   usually   always

When X has a problem outside work that is affecting work, does he/she approach you or some other appropriate person for guidance?

never   sometimes   usually   always

Which statements best describe X regarding the job?

very knowledgeable, keeps up-to-date on all developments	1
very knowledgeable about most areas of work	2
reasonably knowledgeable	3
there are some areas where X is not quite knowledgeable enough	4
not knowledgeable about many aspects of the work	5

Is the overall standard of X's work

very good	1
good	2
average	3
below average	4
poor	5

Fig. 4. Example of a supervisor ratings questionnaire.

Do you often have to criticise X's work
  very often (daily)   1
  often (every week)   2
  average (every month)   3
  sometimes (less than once a month)   4
  almost never   5

Is X efficient with paperwork?
very efficient   very inefficient
    1   2   3   4   5

Is X punctual in the production of reports, etc.?
  very punctual (never late)   1
  reasonably punctual (about 1 in 10 late)   2
  sometimes late (about 1 in 5 late)   3
  often late (more than 1 in 5 late)   4

If you responded 3 or 4, do you know why the reports are late?

Can X work well under pressure?
  very well   1
  average   2
  below average   3

Please rate X on the following characteristics on a scale of 1–5:
1 = displays the quality in most relevant circumstances
2 = usually displays the quality
3 = displays the quality an average amount
4 = sometimes displays the quality
5 = rarely/never displays the quality

relationships with employers   interest in job
decision-making   adaptability
drive   personal appearance
initiative   punctuality
self-control   attendance

Please comment on any particular strengths and weaknesses X has in relation to work.

Strengths:
Weaknesses:

Do you have any suggestions for improvement?

Is it your opinion that X needs further training? If so, what type?

Please comment on X's overall performance.

Please add any further information relevant to this review.

Fig. 4. Contd.

certain useful questions will soon emerge: Why is the value of goods per customer rather low? Why have there been too few new contacts? Why have few of the new contacts been turned into customers?

Forms like this can be designed for any job where objective data is to be had. They are particularly useful when 'confounding' factors have to be taken into account, such as the sales position described here. The important thing is to keep it simple. It is a way of simplifying complicated data to generate useful review questions.

PSYCHOMETRIC TESTING

This is an area much neglected by reviewers. Many organisations fail to see the value of using psychometric tests on their employees. Though many may use certain tests for selection purposes, few are willing to extend this to the review system as a whole.

This is unfortunate because psychometric tests, when used properly, can provide a lot of useful information both for the organisation and for the person being tested. You may not be qualified to select the particular tests required, but an expert can help you. The use of someone trained on a short course in psychometric testing will not be as efficient as using a trained Chartered Psychologist, as the psychologist will have a background of practical and theoretical knowledge that the non-psychologist does not have. The British Psychological Society (BPS) publishes a Register of Chartered Psychologists that should be available in local libraries. If you are referring to this please ensure that the Register is up-to-date. If in doubt, consult the BPS at the address given at the back of this book. Don't use psychologists listed in the *Yellow Pages* or elsewhere unless it indicates they are Chartered.

The best use of psychometric testing

Psychometric tests aren't appropriate for all forms of performance review. There is little point in using what can be quite expensive measures on employees who are simply having their regular performance review. There are two general areas where psychometric tests come into their own, providing information not readily available by other means:

ATTAINMENT OF PREVIOUS OBJECTIVES: SALES PERSONNEL

Reviewee's name:

Position:

Reviewer's name:

Date:

Length of time in post (years):

	TARGET	ACTUAL
Number of customers (N)		
Total value of sales (£)		
Average value of sale per customer (£/N)		
Number of new contacts (Co)		
Number of new customers (Cu)		
Proportion of contacts turned into customers (Cu/Co)		
Size of territory (Ter)		
Number of potential customers (pc)		

Fig. 5. Comparing targets with actual performance.

- when you need to make predictions about future performance

- where the reviewee wishes to find out more about their own future potential.

For example, tests would be appropriate in a promotion or transfer review (predicting who is the best person for the job), and for use in assessing future potential, where tests of vocational interest can help the individual generate ideas for suitable alternative jobs.

Tests have an advantage over other forms of data, such as

supervisor ratings; they are more objective, standardised using large numbers of people, and unbiased (within realistic limits). Test results from properly validated, administered and scored tests are very reliable.

Scope of psychometric tests

Psychometric tests can measure a wide variety of areas. Going back to the person specification, they can indicate general intelligence and special aptitudes, interests, motivation and personality; i.e. four out of the six points mentioned. They are relatively quick to administer (in relation to the information they can provide) and cost-effective.

Choosing the right tests from the ones available

Even if you need to enlist a Chartered Psychologist to select appropriate tests, it is still useful to have some idea of the tests available. There are many tests on the market that are well presented, with glossy brochures and computer-analysed output, but which have not been well constructed and standardised; so it is crucial to be able to tell good tests from bad. The tests are mainly of these types:

- ability tests

- aptitude tests

- personality questionnaires

- interests/values questionnaires

- motivation questionnaires.

Ability tests

These include general ability or IQ (intelligence quotient) tests, which provide useful information about who has the potential to perform well. More detailed information about patterns of specific abilities (e.g. verbal, numerical, spatial) can be obtained using tests specifically designed for these purposes.

Examples
- What is the next number in the series: 1 3 7 15 31?

- Which is the odd one out: biron, porwsra, yenha, gelae

- In each row of words, find a word which means the same as or the opposite of the first word in the row:
      many: ill few down sour
      ancient: dry long happy old

Aptitude tests

These are designed to measure suitability for particular jobs, e.g. sales, mechanical or supervisory roles.

Examples

- (Sales) Look at the following statements. Mark the one that is most like you with an M, mark the one that is least like you with an L.

      My selling is highly personal
      I am a conservative dresser
      I sometimes make price concessions to close a sale
      I have a good feel for people's reactions

- (Clerical) Coding   plastic 25
                        rubber 12
                        china   18

Mark the correct response:
      rubber 25   12   18
      plastic 25   12   18
      china   25   12   18

Personality questionnaires

These provide valuable information about individual characteristics that can be matched to the person specification. They are useful for assessing the reviewee's relationships with others (e.g. which personality characteristics are useful in a team) and how well they will do the job. For instance, perseverance and patience are needed by scientists, managers need to have leadership qualities, sales staff may need to be extrovert.

There is the danger that this kind of test can be faked by individuals to put themselves across in a more favourable light. This can be partly offset in the design of the questionnaire, but the effect of faking cannot be fully dismissed, and information from personality questionnaires should *always* be used along with other methods (interview, ratings, etc.).

Examples

- Do you find yourself the centre of attention at parties?
    usually   sometimes   never

- Do people talk to you about their personal problems?
    often   sometimes   never

- Do you daydream?
    often   sometimes   never

Interest/values questionnaires

These help reveal an individual's basic interests and attitudes across a wide area. How is the individual motivated? How suitable is he/she for different kinds of jobs?

Examples
- Which job would you prefer?
    firefighter
    banker

- Mark the statement that is most like you (M) and least like you (L).
    to have a hot meal at noon
    to get a good night's sleep
    to get plenty of fresh air

Motivation questionnaires

These help determine what it is that motivates people, what drives them to act in the ways they do. Some basic motivators are money, job satisfaction, self-worth and family.

Examples
- True wisdom comes through knowing yourself
    very true   true   false   very false

- Which of the following is the least reliable sign of success in a person's career?
    position of seniority
    rate of promotion
    reputation in the trade or profession
    salary

Which test

Circumstances will dictate which particular tests are most appropriate. The choice of test will depend on factors such as the nature of the performance review, the type of job and the resources of the organisation.

CHOOSING WHAT TYPES OF DATA TO COLLECT

As noted earlier, this depends on several factors – the type of job, its status, and the type of appraisal being carried out. Some examples have been given earlier regarding the use of particular types of data. A number of general remarks can be made.

Importance of current data

> It is *essential* that any job within the organisation has a current job description and person specification.

This is not just for performance review, it is to ensure that the organisation is efficiently staffed, that there are not too many or too few employees, that they are all in the right jobs, and that the jobs are all clearly defined. The job description and person specification should at all times be available to you so that you are knowledgeable about the requirements of the job and the person doing the job.

Job descriptions and person specifications are key sources of data when the review concerns staff movement. This means promotion, transfer or selection (when the job descriptions and person specifications of both relevant jobs will be required), and when the reviewee needs training.

The regular performance review will not need to consider the person specification in any depth if there are no particular performance problems. If there are, the specification can help show why objectives aren't being met. Compare the individual with the person specification and check for discrepancies. If the specification is accurate and the details of the individual are complete, this may well be where the problem lies. The regular performance review may only require measures of performance to compare with set objectives.

Supervisor ratings are useful for most review purposes, though they will not always ask the same questions. For instance, if the reviewee is having vocational assessment, supervisor ratings need not consider present job performance in too much detail. They should concentrate instead on more general elements and on the personality of the reviewee.

Pyschological tests

As mentioned above, psychological tests are useful when the future behaviour of the reviewee needs to be predicted. These situations include:

- promotion

- transfer

- selection

- vocational assessment

- future potential.

Psychological characteristics of individuals do not generally change in the short term. In theory, general intelligence doesn't change at all and personality characteristics are fairly stable. So there is little point in measuring general intelligence or personality at the regular performance review.

The pre-review report

Once all the relevant information or data has been collected, it should be condensed and put together in a **standard format report**.

Both you and reviewee should have a copy of this before the interview. It is important that *both parties* receive the same report. The secret of a good review is openness. Detailed data need not be presented at this stage. If the reviewee is given enormous piles of paper to read it may not get read at all, and simply create ill-feeling towards the review. Detailed data should be available in the review interview in case they need to be referred to.

Too often in situations like this you will receive more information than the reviewee. This puts them at a distinct disadvantage. How can anyone give of their best unless they have equal access to all the information?

Keeping it simple
The report should be simple in form, concise and intelligible to both parties. The information need not take up too much space. There are exceptions of course. An analysis of personality may take up several pages. Ideally the pre-review report should just summarise the findings. The full report can be available at the interview if you need to discuss parts of it. It is important for such details to be open for discussion at the interview as the findings can be controversial.

Similarly, you don't need to include detailed results of supervisor ratings and other ratings. A general summary will do. In the review interview itself you may need to refer to particular comments or ratings, so have these available. The purpose of the review report is to give both parties a general picture of the findings.

The report need not be more than one or two pages long, depending on the job and on the purpose(s) of the review.

Preparing the ground in advance
It is important for both parties to receive the report well in advance of the interview itself so that there is time to digest the contents and prepare responses. It is on the basis of this report that each party decides on the specific **topics** they wish to discuss, or the specific **questions** they wish to ask in the interview. This works both ways. The process is not an interrogation, though some reviewers might prefer it that way. The reviewee needs the information in order to be able to raise their own points.

Keeping a flexible agenda
Reviewees may wish to raise issues that are not strictly 'on the agenda', that do not relate to the purposes of the review as outlined at the outset. This should not deter them from raising the issue, for instance if the organisation is failing to provide adequate canteen facilities, or the work environment is in some way not conducive to health, or their career development is not being helped as they would wish.

It is useful to carry out a further exercise. Once each party has decided on the points they wish to raise in the interview, they should be listed and passed to the other party, so that person can think about their reply. As noted earlier, this system is used in Parliament to good effect, and can work just as well in the appraisal interview.

UNDERSTANDING YOUR OPPOSITE NUMBER

Before an effective interview can take place, it should be ensured that:

- each party understands the purposes of the review
- each party has a copy of the pre-review report and has understood it
- both parties know what issues they wish to raise
- these issues have been given to the other party and that party has considered their responses.

Once all this has been done – and it need not be as difficult as it might appear – then each party will understand what the other wants out of the review interview. This is particularly important to the reviewee. The interview need not now be something to look forward to with foreboding. Nervousness in an interview situation is something that arises partly out of ignorance about what will happen in the interview.

If the report for a member of the sales staff contains information on sales performance, and they have failed to reach their targets, you would doubtless wish to raise this in the interview. If the reviewee is aware of this they can prepare their response. It may be that the poor performance is caused by factors not mentioned on the report such as poor quality samples. If the reviewee has time to think about it properly, they could bring along examples of the goods to show you.

PREPARING FOR THE INTERVIEW

The interview itself should follow a **predetermined plan**. Some reviewers may see this as an unnecessary chore. In fact, it is vital. Rambling interviews generally fail to provide the information required. They often amount to little more than informal chats with no direction or purpose. But for the reviewer who has got this far, who has determined the purposes of the review, collected the data, and compiled a report, it would be unwise not to consider the plan of the interview itself.

The interview consists of a number of stages, depending on the type of review and the number of discussion points. Both parties should be well prepared for the interview, knowing exactly what is going to be discussed, so it should largely be a matter of deciding the order of the discussion points. The general plan should be like this:

1. The performance review is usually different from the selection interview in that both parties are likely to know each other, so the first stage of setting someone at their ease will be different. It is still necessary to help the reviewee relax, as many are nervous about their reviews.

2. Discuss any points arising from the report. Cover these fully before moving on. It is crucial to let the reviewee raise any relevant issues they see as important.

3. Summarise the findings of the report and the discussion so far. Ensure that the reviewee agrees with this summary. This is important to ensure that both parties are still on the same wavelength!

4. Draw conclusions from the review. For the regular performance review this will mean agreeing mutually satisfactory objectives for the coming period. Selection, transfer and redundancy reviews will not have this type of conclusion because you will have to assess everyone before making any decisions. Only preliminary judgements will be made, and these must of necessity be kept from the appraisee.

Within this framework, the discussion of particular topics can be arranged in any sensible order, but don't lose sight of the fact that the interview is basically a conversation between two individuals with needs to be fulfilled, and particular styles of working.

CASE STUDY

Daniel uses psychometric testing

Daniel Jones, managing director in a large computer manufacturing firm, wants to carry out a series of reviews aimed at helping individuals plan their futures within the company. He knows that different types of people are suited to different types of jobs, but he doesn't have any information on how this would relate to his own company. To solve this problem he decides to enlist the services of a psychologist to look at how personality relates to effectiveness at different kinds of jobs.

Daniel arranges for the psychologist to test his staff over three days in one week. Using the results of the test and a measure of job performance, the psychologist will be able to work out which kinds of people are best suited to which particular jobs. The personality tests are duly carried out, the performance data collected, and the results interpreted. Unfortunately, it comes to light that many of the staff did not answer the questions truthfully (there were a number of 'lie questions' on the test), and so the results are invalid.

Daniel then decides to find why people manipulated the results. He finds out that people have been pushed into doing this test without being given any reasons why. A lot of people have assumed that the results are going to be filed and used against them when it comes to obtaining a pay rise or promotion. Because of this they deliberately tried to 'fix' the results to make themselves look good.

Comment
The problem for Daniel is that the employees weren't told before the test of the reasons for it. As soon as someone is asked to take a test they go on the defensive. If not told why they are taking it, they will assume the worst and (particularly with personality tests), they will answer in the way they think the employer wants them to answer.

SUMMARY

In the third part of preparing for the appraisal, we have found that:

- Performance criteria need to be valid and meaningful. They will vary enormously from job to job, and for some jobs are very hard to specify objectively.

- Supervisor ratings can be a good way of obtaining data on the performance of the reviewee, but they must be designed with care.

- **Behaviourally-anchored rating scales** are one way of ensuring ratings are well-defined and accurately completed.

- The reviewee's previous objectives should be clearly related to actual performance; the general level of performance and particular successes and failures can then be seen at a glance.

- Psychometric tests can be a useful source of information for reviews, particularly when information is needed about an individual's potential. They include **ability, aptitude, personality, interests** and **motivation** tests.

- The choice of data depends on the type of job, status of job, and type of review being carried out.

- A pre-review report should contain all relevant data and a copy should be given to both reviewer and reviewee.

- Topics for discussion should be taken from the pre-review report.

- Both parties should be clear about why the review is taking place and what is going to be discussed.

- The interview should follow a clear plan.

EXERCISES

1. BARS provide a relatively objective measure of obtaining supervisors' ratings. From your own experience devise a relevant question and suitable behaviours that could be listed on each point on a five-point scale.

2. If a psychometric test of aptitude was being designed for use on members of your team, what kind of questions do you think would be important?

3. Design a pre-review report form that would be suitable for members of your own management team.

7

Conducting the Interview

This chapter will consider the performance review interview, specifically:

- The timing and setting of the interview.
- The plan of the interview.
- The contents of the final report.

Once the preparation has been carried out the following should have been completed:

— The purposes of the interview have been decided.

— Appropriate data have been collected.

— The information has been disseminated through a report.

— Both parties have been able to raise questions they wish to discuss in the interview.

The interview itself can now go ahead.

INTERVIEW SCHEDULING

There are certain basic guidelines for carrying out interviews of any sort, including reviews. These include the following.

Advance warning
The timing of the interview should be set well in advance (i.e. several weeks) so that both parties can fit their other work around the interview, and there are no clashes with other appointments. Adequate notice will allow enough time for both parties to prepare for the review. It is important that individuals recognise the value of the performance review, that it is perceived to be useful and not just a chore that interferes with their 'real work'. This book has tried to show that the review is a crucial part

of the effective functioning of the organisation. If the system is well designed and well publicised within the organisation, this particular problem should be alleviated.

Picking the right time

If possible, the meeting should be arranged for a **time** (of day, week, month or year) when the reviewee isn't likely to be busy. This isn't always possible but often it is. For example, a mince pie sales executive should not have his review in the last few months before Christmas, the most hectic selling time for mince pies. Neither should the review be carried out just after Christmas, because there probably won't have been time for the organisation to have collected the sales performance figures for the lead up to Christmas. Perhaps March or April would be a good month: after the rush, after the figures have been compiled, but before the next season gets underway. Other jobs, instead of having busy times of the year, have busy times of the month, week or day. The same rule applies.

> **Try and fit the review into a quiet period. It will help the reviewee stop worrying about the work that has to be done. It will also ensure a minimum loss of productivity.**

Upsetting the reviewee's normal work routine should be avoided as much as possible, but it should be emphasised that, in the end, the review *is* part of the normal work routine.

Allowing time for preparation

Do ensure that there is adequate time before the interview date to prepare properly. Complex facts and figures may not be accessed in a few days. It may take weeks, especially if job descriptions have to be devised. On the other hand, the time span shouldn't be too long. It is of little use the reviewee thinking about the review for months, as this may affect their job performance. Performance review is, and should be, a psychologically demanding exercise for the reviewee. Systematic preparation of the kind described in this book should minimise the stress but there is little point in increasing it again by giving the reviewee too long to think about the appraisal. For a regular performance review, the reviewee will know more or less when it is to take place, because it will fall at regular intervals, perhaps the same month every year. But active preparation, from date-setting to data-gathering, should not start too early.

Deciding how long the interview should be

The interview itself needs to be given a long enough **time slot**. Don't try to cram it into a half-hour lunch break. If the interview is too rushed the parties may be unable to cover all the points they wish to raise, and important ones will be skimmed over or missed out entirely. The reviewee may come away frustrated for lack of time to discuss a particular point. This could be a serious demotivator.

The length of the interview will depend on what has to be covered, but, apart from the most basic performance reviews few can be carried out in much under an hour. A session that covers a range of topics, in the detail required, may last up to two hours. If the interview lasts much longer than two hours the participants would probably start to lose their concentration. When setting the date and time for the interview, take this into consideration.

Getting to know each other

If the guidelines described in previous chapters have been followed, there will be quite a lot of contact between yourself and the reviewee before the interview. This will establish the ground rules, what the review is for, and what will happen during the interview, what will be discussed and so forth. Even if you don't know each other before, you should know each other quite well before the interview takes place.

CHOOSING THE PLACE OF INTERVIEW

The interview should be carried out in a quiet warm room, with comfortable chairs, and drinks (not alcohol!) available. Avoid interruptions by visitors or telephones. The image of the reviewer sitting behind a big desk and the reviewee cowering in front of it on a lower chair should be avoided. Confrontation does not help communication. The reviewee may feel cowed and you may find it difficult to forget your power status. The best position is sitting not quite opposite each other, with at the most a low table between you both to put papers on.

CONDUCTING THE INTERVIEW

Both parties should ensure they have the pre-review report to hand, marked with points they wish to discuss. They should both have notes of specific points they wish to raise. Most people cannot be expected to rely on memory to recall all these topics. Both should also have paper on which to jot down points of importance.

The actual structure of the interview cannot be given in detail as (a) different people favour different approaches, and (b) different types of review need different plans. The intent here is to provide general guidelines.

The structure of the interview

The interview should start with a short informal chat on general topics not related to the review, just to ensure both parties are relaxed. The interview proper should then begin with points arising from the report. From this the discussion can broaden to include the other topics to be covered, perhaps the reviewee's strengths and weaknesses, opportunities and problems, achievements, under-achievements, ideas for changes, and possible future objectives. These points should be summarised and agreed, conclusions should be drawn and the session amicably closed.

Points to bear in mind

Certain things need to be kept in mind during the interview:

- What are the purposes of the review? At all times these should be kept in mind and the review should not be allowed to stray from them. This is your responsibility; if you feel that the inter-view is straying, guide it back on course.

- The interview should progress at a sensible rate and cover the issues it is designed to cover. Though issues must be covered in sufficient detail, there may be times when a point is being laboured and little progress made. Control must then be regained (your responsibility) so that the interview can move on to the next point.

- Notes can and should be made by both parties throughout. Afterwards these will form the basis for the final report. Both of you should jot down points discussed, agreements reached and action to be taken. Also note where agreement could not be reached.

- A clear record should be kept of the reviewee's agreed performance objectives for the coming period. It is essential to avoid confusion here. The objectives should be clearly laid out, translatable into sensible performance criteria (so an assessment can be made later), unambiguous and, crucially, achievable.

Communicating with the reviewee

There are almost bound to be some points on which you and the reviewee fail to agree. If this is on performance objectives, an area where there has to be agreement in the end, there should be recourse to a *referee*, someone who can adjudicate and decide what the objectives should be. This person should be someone respected by both parties. It should not be the reviewer, because if you have the ultimate power of decision then the bargaining power of the reviewee will be diminished from the start. The reviewee may lose confidence and trust in you, damaging future relationships. It may still be difficult sometimes, because it could seem to the reviewee that they are powerless, and that objectives are being ordered from above. Of course, this may be necessary in some cases, but avoid it if possible. If the reviewee thinks they have little or no say in the work they have to do, motivation will drop and with it productivity. The individual is important.

Proposing action

You may be in a position to propose action to be undertaken, such as training, but you may not always be able to authorise such action without referring to higher authority. Never make promises you can't keep. If an action has to be authorised by someone else, tell the reviewee this. Explain that you will make a recommendation but that the decision will be made by this third person.

Praising and criticising

Bear in mind throughout the value of **praise** and **criticism**. During the discussion, whenever it is shown that the reviewee has done something praiseworthy, then use praise. It is a great motivator. On the other hand, when the reviewee has done something poorly, then be critical, but constructively so. Don't just say 'Your performance was poor', say 'Your performance was poor. I think it is because of XYZ. What do you think?' The reviewee will accept criticism more readily if it is constructive. If the criticism is not supported by evidence the reviewee is likely to resent the organisation and feel unfairly treated. This will lead to lower productivity.

Closure

By the close of the interview, all discussion points should have been covered in a way acceptable to both parties. As far as possible, the purposes of the review should have been met, conclusions should have been agreed, such as setting objectives for the coming year or agreeing on the reviewee's training needs. The interview should end amicably, even if there have been heated discussions on some matters, and even if agreement wasn't reached on one or a number of points. There is nothing to be gained by taking anger or animosity away from the meeting.

COMPILING THE FINAL REPORT

As soon as possible after the interview, either you or the reviewee should complete the final report. This report should contain details of:

- the purposes of the review

- points discussed

- conclusions reached

- objectives set

- matters that remain unresolved.

The report should then be shown to the other party, who can check it and see whether they agree with the content. There should be space for them to add their own comments, regarding something that has been omitted, or something they disagree with. The report is then signed to show that both parties approve it. It is then forwarded to whoever is authorised to see it, such as the personnel director, the employer, or the person responsible for training. Both the reviewer and the reviewee should keep a copy, and a copy should be filed for future reference by authorised persons.

The report is traditionally written by the reviewer, but this does

PRO-FORMA REPORT FORM FOR THE PURPOSE OF PERFORMANCE REVIEW
This report should be completed as soon as possible after the completion of the interview. All information contained in this report is confidential. It will be seen by no one without the express permission of the reviewee.

Name of reviewee:
Position:
Name of reviewer:

Please complete the following sections in detail.

Performance
Please indicate the areas (a) where reviewee performs exceptionally well, and (b) where any problems might lie.

Rating

Overall performance
  A: Acceptable
  B: Borderline, review in three months
  C: Unacceptable

Personal circumstances
Please include here any aspect of the reviewee's personal situation that after discussion you have agreed are relevant to present and future job performance.

Training needs
Please indicate the areas where you and the reviewee have identified a need for further training, and decisions that have been made regarding that training.

Any other comments
Please include anything here that emerged during the review and has not been covered above.

Reviewee's comments
Please note anything you wish to add to the above.

Signed and dated (reviewer)

Signed and dated (reviewee)

Fig. 6. Example of a report.

not have to be so. If both parties agree the findings of the interview, then a report written by the reviewee has two distinct advantages:

- It acts as a motivator to the reviewee, who is given a real chance to express him or herself and whose views are being taken seriously.

- It ensures that there hasn't been a misunderstanding between the two parties.

Value of the report for future reference

The report can be used for reference in future reviews, as long as it is used with care. It is sometimes argued that previous reports shouldn't be used in this way in case there is an adverse effect. In other words, if the reviewee performed poorly in the past, then the person who reviews them next will be biased and more likely to judge them as doing badly now. As long as care is taken to not make this kind of judgement, by training reviewers to assess data more objectively and not overemphasising the importance of past performance to present performance, the use of previous reports can be helpful. They act as on-going indicators to judge whether the long-term *progress* of the individual is satisfactory.

Confidentiality

There will unfortunately be times when the report has to contain information that the reviewee cannot see. These should be kept to a minimum as secrecy does not help trust. But there are cases where need overrides openness, for instance when the review is for selection or promotion purposes. Here you may have to add a final section after the reviewee has seen the report, that contains specific information and recommendations for whoever is making the selection or promotion.

The report format

Figure 6 gives an example of a report relating to a management post. It gives an idea of how one *might* be structured, but the actual layout will depend on the specific needs of your organisation and the type of review being carried out. For example, if the review is to assess future potential there will need to be a section detailing possible career paths and job roles obtained through discussion with the reviewee.

The format of the report is very important. The use of rating scales is useful because they allow rapid assessments to be made of individuals, and the relationships between individuals – as long as the interpretation is done with care. The comments section relating to each scale is critical, and should be completed in detail so that anyone who reads the report can see why the reviewee obtained a particular rating.

The format suggested in Figure 6 is only one possibility. Different rating scales can be used, different sections will be required. Again, the emphasis is on ensuring that the report is appropriate for your organisational needs.

> **A combination of both quantitative and qualitative information will probably be right for most organisations.**

Both have pros and cons. Rating scales are easy to interpret and help to identify problems, but the information they give is limited, and the actual ratings are open to bias and individual differences in the use of such scales unless adequate training is given. Qualitative information is more subjective, and provides a richer source of information that is particularly likely to be useful when assessing the needs of the reviewee. It will be noted here that the only rating scale on the form relates to performance, and is then only used as an indicator of where problems might lie. This gives the reviewer the information required to take appropriate action, to continuously monitor future performance, to recommend training, etc.

CASE STUDY

Emily's employers misjudge the timing

Emily Bone has been called in for her performance review interview at a particularly busy time. She has received a number of unexpected orders and is under pressure to complete them quickly. On top of the normal pressures associated with rush orders, the shop floor staff are creating difficulties regarding their overtime pay and bonus scheme. They want the bonus to be set at a higher rate than usual to compensate for the extra work and extra hours worked.

Emily, understandably, does not want her review at this time.

She prefers to wait a few weeks until things have calmed down, but 'the powers that be' have set the date and the time and they will not alter it.

In many ways the review system of Emily's company is a good one. It is standardised across the organisation to ensure fair comparisons between individuals in different departments, and the main reviews are carried out by trained staff from the personnel department. Unfortunately there are drawbacks. The system is very rigid and it doesn't allow for situations like Emily's, an unexpectedly busy time. The review system has its own schedules to meet and postponing interviews is seen as a problem to be avoided if at all possible.

Because Emily is under such pressure, her review does not go well. She is ill-prepared and the discussion fails to achieve anything significant. Targets cannot be set, as Emily is not in a position to comment on them. Emily wants to discuss her future, as she hopes to obtain a promotion soon, but again this proves to be impossible because her mind is on the problems in her department. Finally, the reviewer has to agree to another interview at a more convenient date for Emily, so in the end a great deal of time is wasted, both Emily's and the reviewe's.

Comment
The problem here is one of communication. The personnel department is looking to satisfy its own scheduling needs at the expense of Emily, and ends up wasting both parties' time. It would be a simple matter to ask Emily when she would be available.

SUMMARY

In this chapter about the performance review itself the main points have been:

- The interview should take place at a time convenient for both parties.

- There should be adequate time set aside for the review.

- The setting for the interview should be comfortable, and there should be no interruptions.

- The plan of the interview should be followed.

• The review report should contain details of what has been agreed in the interview.

EXERCISES

1. Look at the way you conduct interviews. What are your own strengths and weaknesses as an interviewer? Make a list. Try to look at it from both your point of view and that of the interviewee's.

2. Where do you presently conduct interviews? Is this a good place? Why/why not?

3. Design a suitable report form for your own management team.

8

Following Up and Validating

This chapter will consider following up and validating the performance review. It is important to:

- Quickly follow up recommendations for action.

- Constantly validate the system, using detailed records.

- Avoid unfairness.

- Optimise job satisfaction and organisational efficiency.

An efficient performance review does not end with the performance review interview. There are two further issues to be considered, two important elements to ensure continuity for individual job satisfaction and cost-effectiveness. These are:

- follow up

- validation

The chaper ends with a look at two further issues of importance to individuals and organisations involved in operating performance reviews. These are: why reviews might be unfair; and sources of conflict.

FOLLOWING UP

Any recommendations for action that are made must be followed up.

> **If the conclusion is that the employee needs training, then the right training should be provided as soon as possible.**

There is little point in offering a training course that is needed immediately and then not providing it for twelve months. That may save the cost of training, but it is potentially twelve months' extra productivity wasted, and that productivity should be worth far more than the cost of the training.

This is particularly true in jobs where there is rapidly changing technology. For instance, a computer programmer will need regular training to keep up-to-date on the latest programming languages. It is widely acknowledged that an organisation which fails to keep up with changes in technology is likely to fall by the wayside, but there is little point in keeping up with technology if your employees don't receive appropriate training. Performance review will ensure that training keeps pace with changes in technology.

Making recommendations

If you have only been able to *recommend* training to an authorising person (employer, personnel manager), then make your recommendation quickly, for the reason given above. If for some reason your recommendation is not supported, and the authorising person refuses to fund the training, then the reviewee should be given written notice of this, including the reasons why it was refused. Then, if they wish to, they can appeal against the decision. After all, the decision to recommend training will have been made on detailed objective data, after careful discussion. The reviewee has a right to know the basis on which the authorising person has made their decision. It may be that funds for training are just not available. If so, then it is better to let the reviewee know than to let them think that the organisation doesn't value them as an employee worth training, or even worth keeping informed about what is happening. If the reviewee thinks this, their performance will suffer.

Keeping records

Keep a continuous record of whether performance targets are being attained. Depending on the work being done, this might be a weekly record of objectives set against achievements. This record will encourage reviewees to try to reach targets, and provide useful data for the next review. The supervisor should check this record regularly. Any potential difficulties should be spotted as early as possible, and put right before they get too serious.

The record form should consist, for example, of a checklist of tasks to complete, a sales target to reach, or number of items to produce, where the appropriate category can be marked as achieved and the standard at which it has been completed can be shown.

The importance of follow up

By following up all the recommendations of the review, the organisation will show the individual that he/she is important to it. The review is designed to show this, by not only assessing performance against objectives, but also assessing individual needs and then providing for these needs.

It is crucial that there is **continuity** for the individual and for the organisation in the performance review. Of course, this doesn't fully apply to all forms of review. Selection and transfer, for example, have continuity in the way they are carried out, but in the organisational rather than the individual sense. But continuity is a fundamental part of the regular performance review. It is an integral part of the reviewee's work life. Using data from repeated reviews, performance is assessed over the long term.

The review ensures that the organisation has up-to-date information about the jobs being done and the people that do them. For the reviewee it is a way of knowing that their career is being monitored to make sure it is being developed to the full.

VALIDATING YOUR SYSTEM

Once a review system has been introduced using the guidelines presented in this book, it should not just be used when needed and never examined to check whether it is working properly or not. A car will develop faults if its working parts aren't adjusted or replaced when necessary. It is the same with a performance review. Over time it becomes outdated, through changes in jobs, changes in people and new ways of doing things. This is why your system should be continuously **validated**.

The same basic system should be used throughout your organisation so that comparisons can be drawn between employees' performances. This does not mean that every review will be the same. First, as we have seen, reviews with different purposes are put together in different ways, using different types of data. Different jobs within the organisation will require different reviews. Second, individuals are not the same. They will bring their idiosyncrasies into the design and running of the system. This should not be discouraged, as long as it is kept within reasonable limits, and bias and subjective judgement are kept to a minimum.

Reviews must be carried out in the most efficient manner and the conclusions they draw should be useful both to the organisation and to the individual.

> **Objectives should be attainable, the right person chosen for training, the right person promoted, the individual given job satisfaction.**

The only way to ensure this is constantly to review the system to see what should be changed, where any faults lie and where improvements can be made.

Validation should be an *on-going* process set up at the same time as, and as part of, the review system. This will help dispose of any teething problems. The review system should have regular 'services', it should be validated regularly to ensure it is running smoothly. Over time the organisation changes: in size, structure, the make-up of its employees, its products, its overall philosophy. As these occur, modify the system as necessary. Regular checks will ensure its continuing efficiency.

How to validate the system

In order to validate the review system, detailed **records** need to be kept. These are the standard records that any efficient organisation will keep. They should consist of each employee's **personal file**, including information on background (CV, original application form), history within the organisation (posts held, absenteeism), performance targets and achievements (whether all targets have been attained, if not why not), training and qualifications (job-related academic qualifications will be in background information), and any further relevant data. There should also be detailed and regularly updated job descriptions and person specifications for each job.

The organisation should have someone in the role of **second reviewer**, who is knowledgeable about all aspects of the system and who can carry out the validation.

There are various methods of validating the system. Four essential ones are considered here:

- ask the reviewees whether it is working

**PERFORMANCE REVIEW VALIDITY
QUESTIONNAIRE – REVIEWEE**

Reviewee's name:
Position:
Reviewer's name:
Date:
Date of last review:
Name of previous reviewer:

Please rate the following on a scale of 1 to 5, where:
1 = very acceptable
2 = unacceptable
3 = barely acceptable
4 = acceptable
5 = very acceptable

<u>Rating</u>

The preparation of the reviewer
Your preparation time
The pre-review report
The interview
  did it cover all the necessary issues?
  was it conducted in a professional manner?
The review report
Follow-up

Please answer the following questions in full. Your responses will be treated in strict confidence.

Are you satisfied with your review?   YES   NO
If no, what are the problems you encountered?

Did you get appropriate action on anything that was promised in the review? Please give details.

Any other suggestions or comments about the review procedure.

Fig. 7. Performance review validity questionnaire – reviewee.

- ask the reviewers whether it is working
- assess whether the system predicts performance
- analyse the completed review forms.

Asking the reviewees

The first two methods involve using a standard questionnaire (different for reviewee and reviewer – see below). The reviewees questionnaire should contain questions about the competence of the reviewer, whether the information obtained before and during the interview was complete and accurate, whether performance objectives were set at a reasonable level, and perhaps most importantly, whether intended actions arising out of the interview were followed up rapidly and efficiently. An example of a questionnaire that might be given to the reviewee is shown in Figure 7.

The combination of quantitative scales and qualitative comments should get the maximum information from the reviewee. Action should be taken on any question where they have expressed discontent. This may mean interviewing them to find out more details, interviewing the reviewer, or looking at report forms.

Asking the reviewers

The questionnaire designed to be completed by the reviewer is slightly different from the one administered to the reviewee. An example of such a form is shown in Figure 8.

Does the system predict performance?

The next validation method involves checking the various types of data. If the ways of collecting data are valid, then they should predict what they are supposed to about employees. For instance, supervisor performance ratings should correlate with more objective performance criteria (such as sales figures, productivity); psychological tests should predict future performance.

Predictive validity is important when the review system is used for job changes, transfer or promotion. Records are kept of the reviewee's predicted performance. Predictions are made by using data such as psychological test scores, ratings on previous job, productivity on previous job. At some point in the future (perhaps a year hence), actual performance on the new job is measured. A correlation is obtained between predicted and actual performance. The higher the correlation, the higher the validity of

**PERFORMANCE REVIEW VALIDITY
QUESTIONNAIRE – REVIEWER**

Reviewer's name:
Position:
Date:

Details of reviews carried out in last month:

Date   Reviewee's name   Purpose of review

Continue on a separate sheet if necessary.

Please rate the following on a scale of 1 to 5, where:
   1 = very unacceptable
   2 = unacceptable
   3 = barely acceptable
   4 = acceptable
   5 = very acceptable

The ratings are for general comments relating to reviews carried out in the last month.

<u>Rating</u>

Time available for preparation
Access to relevant data
How well the reviewee has prepared
Site for interview
Pre-review report
Review report form
Follow-up

Please answer the following questions in full. Your responses will be treated in strict confidence.

Are you happy with the review procedure?   YES   NO
If no, please give details of the problems you encountered.

Were you able to fulfil any promises relating to the review? If not, please indicate why.

Any other suggestions or comments about the review procedure.

Fig. 8.   Performance review validity questionnaire – reviewer.

the review system (or at least that aspect that predicts future performance). In this way predictive validity is extremely valuable.

Analysing the completed forms

This involves checking the review forms to ensure they are being completed in a manner that is fair to all groups and individuals, and that the information they contain is reasonable and helpful given the circumstances of the reviewee and the organisation. The responses on review forms should not contain assessments that are unfair, nor should they contain irrelevant information, e.g. in the personal information section.

If the size of the organisation warrants it, the second reviewer should interview a sample of reviewees, using the completed review form, working through the form to ensure the reviewee is satisfied with what it contains. This may help identify areas reviewees are dissatisfied with even if they didn't note it on the completed form.

The second reviewer will be able to pick out other problems by comparing a sample of reports from different departments completed by different reviewers. Where rating scales are used the second reviewer can establish that they are being used in a similar manner by different reviewers. For example, on a 5-point scale some people tend to use the middle, others tend to use the extreme scores more. This can be alleviated by training, and by using BARS (see page 88).

Checking the system

Validation is an essential part of the review system. Without proper validation, there is no way of establishing whether the sytem is working well, whether it is fair, and whether it is achieving its objectives. If it isn't doing these things then it is of little value either for the organisation or for the individual employee. Validation is cost-effective because it can quickly help to identify any problems.

HOW PERFORMANCE REVIEW CAN BE UNFAIR

Unfairness can arise at any point in the review system. It is essential to try to minimise unfairness.

Even those people who consider themselves extremely fair-minded have many biases and prejudices about others and towards ideas. This can affect how the review works. If we didn't classify people using **stereotypes**, which introduce systematic bias and prejudice, then we would find it difficult to put order into the way we look at the world. Stereotyping is the process of grouping essentially heterogeneous people into homogeneous categories, such as the employee who is a member of a union being seen as a potential trouble-maker when there is no evidence for this. This is unfair, but because stereotyping is a 'natural' phenomenon, it is difficult to eliminate.

Unfairness is in many cases trivial, but it can sometimes lead to serious consequences. Common stereotypes include **race, sex role** and **social class**.

First impressions

Linked to sterotypes is the notion of 'first impressions'. The first time we meet people we have a psychological need to classify them as quickly as possible. So we latch on to a particular characteristic, or look, and link that to ones that, in our personal view of the world, belong to some stereotypical group. Once that characteristic has been identified, then the person is assumed to have all the other characteristics of that stereotype.

Example

To take a simple and rather unsubtle example, a manager may wrongly imagine that anyone with a non-standard southern English accent is lower in intelligence, tends to have less educaton and has poorer leadership qualities than someone with a standard accent. Though the manager may not *consciously* think in this way, they may *act* on the stereotype in the performance review and, perhaps, fail to suggest that the reviewee is put forward for promotion. This manager is behaving in a way common to us all, that is, we act on *assumptions* that we have made without our even knowing that we have made them. This sort of problem can be avoided when acting in the role of reviewer – or for that matter the reviewee – by careful analysis of the data available about a person, not the 'data' that you are inventing because you are using stereotypes. Awareness of stereotyping and its effects can itself reduce these effects because we can learn to act on the objective data, not our subjective judgements.

The halo effect

Another form of unfairness is called the 'halo effect'. This occurs when you know that the reviewee has done particularly well in one area of work, and so you assume that all other areas of the job are being done just as well. For instance, the reviewee may have done an excellent piece of work and received a bonus for it. You may fall into the trap of noting this particular piece of work and emphasising it so much that other areas of performance are ignored. But this may be the only bit of very good work the appraisee has done, and there may be real problems in other areas.

The review interview shouldn't just concentrate on praising the good work; it should also bring out the reasons for poor performance so that something can be done about it. Perhaps the reviewee in the above example, acting quite naturally, will try to focus discussion on this good piece of work to avoid being questioned on failings in other areas.

The halo effect also works in reverse. An otherwise competent individual may be over-criticised because of a single shoddy piece of work. Again it can work over the long term. The individual may get an unjustified reputation as a poor worker. This has the added danger of turning into a **self-fulfilling prophecy**. If the individual is viewed by others as incompetent, then this perception itself may cause him or her to perform incompetently.

IDENTIFYING SOURCES OF CONFLICT

No matter how open, fair and equal the review system is designed to be, power games may be played between the two parties, who can often see themselves in some sort of organisation versus employee conflict. Power games occur in reviews because the roles of the reviewer and reviewee as 'boss' and 'subordinate' are temporarily suspended; both parties may be vying for position in the 'equal' roles.

Conflict arises from certain other sources:

- Within the reviewee, who may fear that the object is to decide who to dismiss, or who to withhold bonuses or pay rises from.

- Within the reviewer, who may believe the reviewee is trying to hide information.

- Within the organisation itself, the climate of which may foster conflict more than co-operation.

Conflict does not help the effective review system. Performance reviews should be run in a spirit of co-operation rather than conflict, with both parties working together to solve problems.

Designers of performance review systems need to find ways of minimising potential conflict, and one good way is via training. If both parties are aware of possible sources of conflict, and how they harm the process, they are more likely to try to avoid them.

CASE STUDY

Mark's training needs are not followed up

Mark Blake's review was quite useful, or so he thought immediately afterwards. He had discussed with Martin Hale, his reviewer, a number of problems he has had recently. Mark works for a car manufacturer that believes in a broad-based training for its junior managers. Following this philosophy, Mark has recently moved from production to sales to widen his experience. Unfortunately, he has found it hard to adapt. He is nervous when meeting new people, often making mistakes in what he says. This didn't matter in production, even though he was meeting people all the time, as they were usually the same people. In sales it is different, Mark has to meet new people every day, and if he makes a mistake he may lose a sale.

The first three months were not very good in comparison with other new members of the sales staff. Martin was very sympathetic to Mark's case in the review and they both realised something needed to be done about it.

'Assertiveness training, that's what you need,' said Martin. Mark agreed. This was included in the report, to be carried out as soon as possible.

After the review, Mark carried on making mistakes in his work, improving little with practice. He was waiting for the training, but it didn't come. He contacted Martin, who said, 'I'm sorry. I'd informed personnel, they should have dealt with it. I'll get on to them straightaway.

Mark again waited and nothing happened. Again he contacted Martin, who again apologised and promised to 'get it sorted out'.

Mark eventually waited six months before he finally got the training, by which time he had wasted six months in a job he didn't like and wasn't very good at. By the time he had the training it was time for him to move on, and so any benefits gained from the training would not benefit sales.

Comment
This situation shows how easy it is for action promised at a review not to happen. The firm has a very good management programme that involves training and broad job experience, but in this instance it failed due to a lack of communication between the relevant departments. The potential loss is significant. Apart from the loss of sales in the period Mark did not have his training, there is the possibility that he will become disillusioned with the company and either fail to live up to his potential, or find a job elsewhere with a company that keeps its promises.

SUMMARY

This chapter has suggested that:

- Any recommendations for action made in the performance review interview should be followed up quickly.

- The performance review system needs constant validation. Detailed records must be kept, and the same system used throughout the organisation.

- Ways of validating the system include: asking the participants for their thoughts, checking whether the system predicts future performance, and analysing the completed reports.

- Unfairness should be avoided. Unfairness includes stereotyping, relying on first impressions, acting on false assumptions, the halo effect.

- The twin purposes of performance reviews are to optimise individual job satisfaction and organisational efficiency.

- If the organisation satisfies the needs of the individual, the individual is likely to satisfy the needs of the organisation.

EXERCISES

1. In your own organisation, how could follow up procedures be made more effective?

2. What would be the best ways of validating a performance review procedure in your own organisation?

3. In what ways could you minimise unfairness in your own review procedures?

9

Present Thoughts and Future Directions

This chapter will consider:

- The state of performance review.
- Alternative sources of data.
- The validity of rating scales.
- Reviewing professional and scientific staff.
- The problem of performance review.

ASSESSING THE STATE OF PERFORMANCE REVIEW

Research continues in the field of performance review. This chapter considers some of the issues confronting designers of review systems and practitioners at the present time. Since the 1980s more and more organisations have introduced performance review systems, with twin intentions of creating an effective working environment for individual employees and increasing organisational productivity (however that is assessed). It is not only private sector organisations that use performance review, in the last 15 years it has become commonplace for public sector organisations to implement complex review systems.

Performance review is big business; but big business does not always mean good business. Many of the systems in place at the present time, while they may have been introduced with good intentions and may be well-designed, do not always work. In 1949 Thorndike specified four criteria for effective assessment:

- validity
- reliability
- freedom from bias

- and practicality.

This book has been an attempt to address these criteria, to help you design and implement a practical and effective performance review system. Unfortunately, even when there are the best of intentions a system will not work if the people concerned do not make it work. In order for it to work the people involved – must have faith in the system. A study in North America estimated that over 90 per cent of organisations used some kind of performance review, but that fewer than 20 per cent of these are conducted effectively. It is hoped that by using this book you will have the means to implement a good performance review system and apply the principles effectively. In order to do this you need the support of your staff.

FINDING ALTERNATIVE SOURCES OF DATA

In the last few years there has been a lot of work carried out into the role of the reviewee's colleagues and how they can contribute to the review.

Self-review

A lot of research has looked at the appropriateness of reviewees assessing themselves. There are several advantages to this method for the reviewee:

- It can enhance their sense of dignity and self-respect.

- It is likely to increase their commitment to organisational and personal goals.

- It will be an effective motivator.

Unfortunately there is a downside to the use of self-ratings. Studies comparing self- with supervisor ratings have indicated that – unsurprisingly – employees consistently rate themselves higher than do supervisors. This is particularly true for managerial and professional groups compared to manual workers. Apart from understandable self-enhancement, perhaps this indicates the difficulties inherent in assessing jobs that are essentially ambiguous in nature.

Peer reviews

While some studies show that assessments by peers are more valid than other forms of assessment, it is often found that there are systematic biases in these ratings. Individuals will rate others they perceive as similar to themselves higher than those they perceive as dissimilar. Again, there are differences between occupations and between tasks. Those tasks which are easily quantifiable are usually peer-assessed more reliably than ambiguous measures. The problem with the research here is that there is a confusion between who is doing the assessment and the method of assessment. Differences are often found when using unreliable criteria, as is the case generally.

Research has shown that peer assessments are more stable than supervisor assessments, and that they are more likely to focus on the reviewee's performance than on effort. They are also good at making accurate predictions regarding future performance.

Subordinate reviews

As stated in an earlier chapter, very few organisations actually use subordinate reviews. There are two reasons why this may be so. First, the approach is incompatible with the management styles of many organisations, where there is still a clear distinction between management and workers. Second, there is a fear that subordinate reviews may undermine managerial power.

On the other hand, there are good reasons why subordinate reviews should be carried out. First, subordinates are in a position to observe managerial behaviour. Second, the use of multiple assessments will help eliminate the bias arising when only one rater is used. Third, a formal system is compatible with modern models of commitment to and involvement in the organisation which many managers advocate as a way of increasing productivity. It has been suggested that there are specific keys that will make subordinate ratings work:

- participative management style
- rater anonymity
- behaviour-specific items.

If subordinate ratings are to be used then the reviewers should ensure the subordinates are aware of the supervisor's job specification. If they aren't, then how will they be in a position to make valid assessments? It also follows that subordinates should only make assessments on supervisor behaviours that they are in a position to observe. It is also crucial that subordinates receive training in the use of such scales. Finally, subordinate ratings should not be used alone, but in conjunction with other forms of data, such as supervisor ratings, or performance criteria.

The present climate may still not be ready for subordinate reviews, though surveys have demonstrated that the majority of managers would welcome or at least accept such ratings. Of course, what managers say and how they behave may be very different things!

THE VALIDITY OF RATING SCALES

The problem with using all kinds of rating scales is that they are usually found to be subject to systematic errors in the form of a halo effect (see page 124). Whoever completes the scale, the reviewee is likely to be rated higher than their true performance merits. There are ways of checking whether a particular rater or rating scale is subject to the halo effect. One way is to use psychometric tests that measure similar behaviours and then compare scores. An alternative is to use various statistical procedures. But neither of these are ideal solutions.

Counteracting bias

The other potential problem with rating scales is that there could be bias against members of particular groups, e.g. sex or race. Research in this area is unclear. Some studies suggest such bias exists, others say it doesn't. But within any performance review system, care must be taken to ensure such errors don't occur. The use of rating scales, no matter how effectively carried out, always has an element of subjective interpretation. It is in the end the individual's subjective interpretation as to whether to award a 2 or a 3. For this reason it is often useful to include a qualitative element, to allow the individual an opportunity to express their views in more detail, whether as part of an interview, or as an open-ended question on a questionnaire.

REVIEWING PROFESSIONAL AND SCIENTIFIC STAFF

It is only fairly recently that many organisations have started to appraise professional staff. Performance review was originally used almost exclusively for managerial staff, and the problems with designing review systems were related to the difficulties of assessing managers. Performance review then began to include other grades of staff, such as shopfloor workers. The problems with reviewing these groups are often less than for managerial staff because performance can often be measured more objectively and with validity. There are likely to be more difficulties associated with reviewing professional and scientific staff, at least in part because 'performance' is often an even more nebulous concept than for managers.

Considering the difficulties

To take the example of an academic scientist, measuring their performance can be very difficult. The product of science is knowledge, which is very difficult to quantify. Unfortunately the present political climate requires objective quantification of the output of a scientist, so we have the situation where academics are being assessed on the number of research papers they produce in terms of the number of pages written. This kind of criterion is proven to be nonsensical when we observe that Einstein's original exposition of his special theory of relativity was a one-page research note. This invalidates the whole notion of objective measurement in this area. The measurement itself may be accurate, but counting the number of pages written does not give an indication of the quality of the work.

Creativity

A further problem regarding quality of output in the area of scientific research is that of creativity. Creativity does not appear to order. A scientist may spend years apparently not achieving a great deal and then suddenly come up with an important theoretical contribution. If a review system had demanded particular 'objective' output through these years then perhaps the scientist would not have been able to have the intellectual space to generate this theory.

This is a difficult matter, because while the above is true, the converse is also true. In an academic environment there are likely to be individuals who function as 'hangers on', who in actuality produce very little. Though it might be argued that this is a small price to pay for the contributions others will make.

Performance indicators

This may apply to other professions. Again there are problems relating to the measurement of performance. Should lawyers be measured on the number of cases won? Should medical doctors be measured on the number of patients cured? This is clearly absurd, though in certain areas of the public sector (e.g. health and education) this is now to some extent occurring.

Organisations and individuals should resist this. There are often situations where there can be no objective performance indicators. Doctor A may cure more patients than doctor B, but is this because doctor B has better preventative health procedures set up? Or is it because there are more 'ill' people in doctor B's area? Or is it because A used some radical new treatment approaches that are more effective than those used elsewhere? Or is it because doctor A had a higher proportion of curable patients than doctor B? Or is it because doctor A has a better bedside manner? The list of questions could go on and on. This example is included to demonstrate the absurdity of trying to quantify something inherently unquantifiable.

Measuring professional performance

The performance of many professionals is best measured through peer review. It is the group that is in an ideal position to determine the effectiveness and the needs of the individuals involved, and as we have seen, peer review can be at least as effective as supervisor measures. The peer review system is now becoming widely used in the university sector, where each member of an academic department will be reviewed by another member of the department. Clearly, while this might be very effective, there may be problems with a 'you rub my back and I'll rub yours' kind of attitude. The review system needs to be designed with this possibility in mind. A formal system, with detailed feedback, and a specific individual with overall responsibility for the functioning of the system, will help professionals to come to terms with the concept of performance review.

THE PROBLEM WITH PERFORMANCE REVIEW

It has been argued that performance review is one of the seven deadly sins afflicting managers because it inappropriately attributes variation in performance to the individual employee rather than to problems at a higher organisational level. The effect of this is to shift the blame for problems onto individuals rather than to look at what is wrong with the way the organisation is set up.

This kind of problem can jeopardise not only the review system itself, but the morale of the workforce, particularly if they feel they are being unfairly criticised. If this happens, the main reasons for having the review, increased productivity and increased job satisfaction, will be lost.

> **In order to be effective, the appraisal system must take account of the philosophy and structure of the organisation at a level higher then the individual.**

Finally, in organisations where there is a strong emphasis on teams, consideration should be given to running reviews for the team as a whole rather than for individual team members. This makes more sense where performance is assessed on the basis of teams rather than individuals.

CONCLUSIONS

If the guidelines laid out in this book are followed, then performance review will perform a useful function as a critical part of the organisation. On the other hand, reviews have little value if they are not designed properly. If they are not valid the organisation will simply be throwing money away, wasting time and resources on a system that doesn't do what it is supposed to do, optimise organisational efficiency and individual job satisfaction.

If the review system is well-designed it can provide most useful information for the organisation on a range of topics, from assessing performance to choosing the best candidate for promotion.

> **The review is used as a method of assessing individual performance within the organisation. There are two main purposes: to ensure that the right person is in the right job and doing it to a suitable standard, and to ensure that the person doing the job has a high degree of job satisfaction and fulfilment.**

Too many review systems only consider the first purpose, at best paying lip-service to the second. In modern society there is a growing awareness of the value of people, that they mean more than short-term profit.

- The individual must be motivated to work with the organisation. Performance review can enable the organisation to find out and provide for the needs of its individual employees.

- If the organisation satisfies the needs of the individual, the individual will satisfy the needs of the organisation.

SUMMARY

In this chapter we have considered:

- general issues relating to performance review
- alternative data collection methods
- validity of rating scales
- reviewing professional and scientific staff
- the problem with performance review.

EXERCISES

1. How would you answer the claim by professional staff that they don't need performance review?

2. Thinking about your own organisation, how could peer or subordinate ratings work?

3. How would you distinguish between work problems associated with the individual employee and problems associated with the organisation?

10

Examining More Case Studies

This chapter contains a series of case studies illustrating performance review systems in different organisations. Each case study consists of:

- Summary task analysis, job description and person specification forms.

- An outline of the review system in use, including its good and bad points, and how it might be improved.

The jobs included here are chosen to illustrate a variety of roles. The issues discussed apply to most, if not all, jobs. The jobs are:

- veterinary nurse

- workshop foreman

- accounts clerk

- technical manager

- university lecturer

- supermarket cashier.

VETERINARY NURSE

Task analysis
Job title: veterinary nurse
Company: Elmingbury Veterinary Hospital
Supervisor's name: all partners of practice
Appraiser's name: Helen Robinson (veterinary surgeon)

Task	Knowledge/skills	Aptitudes	Personality
Pre-operation preparation	Anaesthesia Sterilisation		Practical

Assisting in surgery	Theatre nursing	Manual dexterity	Attention to detail
Post-op care	General nursing		Cope in emergency
Laboratory analysis	Basic scientific skills	Observation Analytical	Patience
Ordering drugs	Drug knowledge	Clerical/ arithmetic	
Take/develop X-rays	Radiology		Conscientious
Field trips	General nursing		Practical Adaptable
Reception	Filing	Clerical	Friendly Sociable

It will be seen from this task analysis that not all categories are completed. This is largely because particular characteristics cannot be stated for many tasks. The important thing is that *all* the tasks the nurse does are included in the list, and any **essential** skills, aptitudes or personality characteristics are included.

Job description

Job title: veterinary nurse.

Department: NA.

Responsible to: head veterinary nurse.

Responsible for: trainee nurses.

Number employed on this work: 8.

Position from which candidates for this job might come: none internal, usually school-leavers.

Avenues of promotion: head veterinary nurse.

Purpose/objects of work: to assist veterinary surgeon in all aspects of her work, especially in the preparation, care and after-care of animals.

Main duties/activities: general veterinary nursing, laboratory, surgery, drug dispensing/ordering, dealing with enquiries.

Forms/equipment: order book for drugs, case history cards, veterinary care equipment.

Contacts: daily contact with team of veterinary surgeons, nurses, members of public.

Discretion: can vary only within limited parameters, determined by instructions of veterinary surgeons.

Checking: frequent, carried out by all veterinary surgeons.

Supervision required: receive daily instructions on diagnostic matters. All such decisions are the sole responsibility of veterinary surgeon.

Supervision given: limited authority to assign general duties to trainee nurses.

Other responsibilities: on call evenings and weekends on rota with other nurses. Delivery and collection of animals and laboratory samples.

Working conditions: two years training, rate of pay on qualification £4.80 per hour basic.

Personal requirements: practicality, common sense, hard-working, acceptance that veterinary nursing is a way of life.

The task analysis has helped the reviewer design the job description, though information from other sources is also used, such as personnel records and information from the veterinary surgeons. The reviewer, by combining the information from the task analysis and the job description, can now complete the person specification.

Person specification

Essential	Desirable	Conflicting
Qualifications		
3 GCSEs	English Language	
	Biology	
Intelligence/aptitudes		
Average general	Manual dexterity	
ability	Clerical aptitude	
	Analytical	
Personality		
Common sense	Cheerful	Fear of blood/dirt
Practical	Stable	Tender-minded
Hard-working		Absent-minded
Interests		
Animals	People	
Biology		
Motivation		
Love of animals		Money
Caring		

Appearance/circumstances

Few family pressures   Concern with looks

How the review system works

The review system for the veterinary nurses in this hospital consists of a regular performance review every six months. As it is a small organisation, most review work is carried out on an informal day-to-day basis. This does not obviate the need for the regular formal review. Reviews for the nurses are all carried out by the same veterinary surgeon (who is responsible for all general personnel issues), and they are spread through the year so she isn't overloaded with too many reviews at once.

This is a reasonably good system for an organisation such as this. Assigning responsibility to a single veterinary surgeon is useful because it makes for consistency in how the interviews are carried out, as long as the reviewer is fair to all the nurses. It is particularly useful to have performance reviews every six months because most veterinary nurses are relatively young females whose lives may be changing rapidly.

In small organisations staff review is carried out just on a *day-to-day* basis, with *no* formal interview. While this saves a great deal of time in a busy practice, it may mean that the practice is not making the best use of staff, and staff discontent may go unnoticed until it is too late.

The data collected for the performance review consists of a supervisor questionnaire, obtained from all the veterinary surgeons. Each surgeon is asked the same series of questions, specifically:

- Is the reviewee efficient in surgery?

- Does the reviewee competently carry out all duties regarding pre- and post-operative care?

- Does the reviewee carry out other duties efficiently (X-rays, field trips, laboratory analysis, etc.)?

- Are there any areas where the reviewee is deficient? Could this be rectified by further training?

- Is the reviewee's general attitude to work acceptable?

- Have you any general comments to make about the reviewee?

This questionnaire is short, which is very useful because veterinary surgeons (like most groups) typically do not like filling in forms. One problem that may arise is that the reviewer is one of the surgeons. This is a problem typical of smaller organisations, where **objectivity of judgement** is difficult because everyone knows each other very well and there may be personal favourites and petty animosities. The reviewer must remain objective by taking into account the general views of the veterinary surgeons. As data is obtained from all the veterinary surgeons, any personal dislikes should be alleviated by the general picture.

The problem with this kind of data is that it is difficult to make clear judgements. The surgeons will seldom all make exactly the same comments about a particular reviewee. The reviewer has to be careful to form a balanced judgement about the reviewee's need for training, general competence, or attitude to work.

It may be more efficient if the supervisors were asked to fill in rating scales regarding these questions. It would certainly make it easier for the reviewer to draw conclusions about the views of the veterinary surgeons. Behaviourally-anchored rating scales would be best, to obtain the maximum consistency of judgement.

There is no standardised report form. Any comments made by the reviewer are simply entered on a piece of paper in the reviewee's personnel record file. This piece of paper rarely includes any comments made by the supervisor, or any of the reviewee's own comments, but simply any conclusions drawn by the reviewer.

Clearly, there is a need for a report form that is standardised and thus comparable between reviewees. It should contain details of work performance as assessed by the supervisor questionnaire, plus:

- details of any objectives, both organisational and personal, for the coming period

- details of the conclusions reached by the reviewer after the interview

- a section for any comments the reviewee wishes to add.

The form should be signed by both the reviewer and the reviewee to ensure it has been read and accepted by both.

This system is not validated in any way. A second reviewer should therefore be appointed. This would be one of the other veterinary surgeons, who can ask the employees whether they are satisfied with the system, and check the conclusions drawn by the reviewer from the supervisor questionnaire.

Unfortunately, though the system works reasonably well for the other nurses, the head nurse rarely receives her performance review. The veterinary surgeons do not see the need for it. She has been with the hospital for a number of years, starting as a trainee nurse and working her way up. The veterinary surgeons are perfectly happy with her performance, and, as she has never complained, they assume she is happy in her work. This type of assumption can be dangerous, as there may be underlying problems that develop over time, relating to work or personal life.

A problem that could emerge is that the head nurse is unable to obtain promotion within the organisation. The only way to obtain more status would be to move to a larger veterinary hospital. If the veterinary surgeons are happy with her performance they should ensure she has enough job satisfaction to want to stay. This may mean altering her conditions of service, perhaps a pay increase, reducing her hours of work, changing the tasks she has to do, or (if she has a family) reducing the time she has to be on call at evenings and weekends. The best way to ensure she isn't becoming dissatisfied is not to wait for her to say so – she may never say anything – but to hold a formal review where this type of problem is discussed as a matter of course.

Conclusion
Although the hospital has a reasonable performance review system, there are some relatively minor changes that could improve it considerably. They would not be too expensive or time-consuming to introduce, but they would lead to considerable benefits to the practice.

WORKSHOP FOREMAN (CAR MECHANIC)

Task analysis
Job title: foreman
Department: workshop
Company: Banders of Bletchley
Reviewee's name: Geoff Priggen
Supervisor's name: Daniel Johnson
Reviewer's name: Richard Kilburn

Task	Knowledge/skills	Aptitudes	Personality
Maintenance of vehicles	City & Guilds Motor Vehicle Technology	Mechanical Manual dexterity	
Supervising technicians		Leadership Motivating Verbal	Sociable
Diagnosis of faults		Analytical	Patient

The term 'maintenance of vehicles' covers a host of tasks, from routine servicing of vehicles, to changing engines, to bodywork repairs. For this particular job the City & Guilds qualification assumes that the individual will be competent in all these tasks. 'Diagnosis of faults' is included as a separate task because it involves an intellectual aptitude, analytical ability, that is not crucial to simply maintaining vehicles. Of course, a mechanic will always be involved with diagnosing faults, but it is useful to have this separate category so the reviewer can see in which areas particular abilities are needed.

Job description
Job title: foreman.

Department: workshop.

Responsible to: service manager.

Responsible for: 6 workshop technicians.

Number employed on this work: 1.

Position from which candidates for this job might come: workshop technician.

Avenues of promotion/transfer from this position: service manager.

Purpose/objects of work: maintenance of motor vehicles and diagnosis of faults.

Main duties/activities: as above, plus supervision of technicians and quality control check.

Forms/equipment: quality control forms, use of diagnosis machinery.

Contacts: constant contact with technicians, daily contact with service manager, regular contact with public.

Discretion: assigning duties to technicians.

Checking: work is checked weekly at random.

Supervision required: none.

Supervision given: assigning and checking work of technicians and dealing with minor disciplinary problems.

Other responsibilities: dealing with complaints from public, ordering parts, checking machinery, auditing.

Working conditions/conditions of service: training for the basic job of technician is three years. Supervisory status is only obtained after a number of years' shopfloor experience. The post is salaried, £17,000 a year.

Personal requirements: City & Guilds qualification in motor vehicle technology. Self-reliant, sociable, practical.

Person specification

Essential	Desirable	Conflicting
Qualifications		
City & Guilds	GCSEs	
Intelligence/aptitudes		
Manual dexterity	Analytical	
Mechanical		
Personality		
Resourceful	Sociable	Absent-minded
	Patient	
Interests		
Mechanical		
Motivation		
Appearance/circumstances		
Smartly dressed		

There is no comment under 'motivation' as the person in this job need not be motivated by any of the usual things – money, status, friends, etc. In cases such as this, where there are no definite characteristics to be included, the space should be left blank, as including something that is not relevant will be misleading.

How the review system works

The performance review system at Banders of Bletchley (a garage which is part of a national chain) covers all technicians, including the workshop foreman. The service manager carries out reviews annually. The data used for the general technicians consist of written comments provided by the workshop foreman. The interview for the workshop foreman is quite informal; the reviewer doesn't bother obtaining any data beforehand, and the interview itself is little more than a friendly chat. The only problems the service manager knows about concerning the foreman are those he has heard 'on the grapevine'.

Clearly, the system at Banders has a number of faults. While the supervisor doesn't actually carry out the reviews of the technicians, he is responsible for providing all the data the reviewer will use. If he has problems in his relationships with any of the technicians, there may be an adverse effect on the way he writes the comments. This is a very subjective and one-sided way of collecting data. The reviewer should, as well as obtaining supervisor ratings, assess the technicians on other measures of performance: number of mistakes made, time taken to complete tasks, interaction with the public, and so on.

The review for the workshop foreman is worse. This is not really a review at all. It is just an informal chat. If the foreman has anything about his performance to hide, he will probably succeed in doing so. There need to be other ways of obtaining data, ratings from the technicians (subordinate ratings), number of mistakes made, etc.

In order to improve the system and the overall functioning of the garage, the reviewer should introduce **standard methods** of assessing performance. Records should be kept of how all the technicians, the foreman included, perform. These forms can include measures of, for instance, number and type of errors made, and time taken to complete work.

The results of the review are not shown on a standard form to be referred to at a future date. The review report form is essential, as the results of the interview are only known to the reviewer, and if they are not recorded they will be forgotten. The standard form can be quite short, with questions relating to:

- performance measures
- explanations of good/poor performance
- future objectives
- needs of the reviewee.

The garage is part of a national chain, but there is no standard system used throughout the chain. The responsibility for reviews is left solely to the service manager. As attitudes of service managers will vary enormously, standards of review at different garages will vary in a similar fashion. If individuals wish for promotion within the organisation, perhaps via transfers to other garages, some will be at an unfair disadvantage simply because their service manager showed little interest in performance review, and so produced very little performance data on the employees.

Conclusion

The system in this organisation needs a thorough overhaul at national level. There should be a common policy for appraisals (formal reviews, with objective ways of collecting data, standard report forms, etc.), and service managers should undergo thorough training in review techniques.

ACCOUNTS CLERK

Task analysis

Job title: accounts clerk
Department: accounts
Company: Street & Co
Reviewee's name: Cherilyn Heale
Supervisor's name: Jane Oldfield
Reviewer's name: Stephen Claxton

Task	Knowledge/skills	Aptitudes	Personality
General accounts	Basic accountancy	Numerical	
Customer liaison	Workings of company		Sociable Friendly
Word processing	Typing/shorthand	Manual dexterity	Conscientious
Reception telephone			Polite

Job description

Job title: accounts preparation clerk.
Department: computer room.

Responsible to: John Street (Partner).

Responsible for: NA.

Number employed on this work: 3.

Positions from which candidates for this job might come: accounts department, purchase/sales, ledger clerks.

Avenues of promotion/transfer from this position: none within organisation.

Purposes/objects of work: monthly/annual analysis of accounts.

Main duties/activities: preparing and inputting accounts, reception, word processing, customer liaison.

Forms/equipment: personal computer skills, word processing, spreadsheet, accounts packages.

Contacts: daily with partners, other staff, daily with customers.

Discretion: none. All work produced to standard format.

Checking: all work double-checked by other clerks, and also partners.

Supervision required: all work authorised by one or other partner.

Supervision given: all staff in computer room on same level, advice and help given to each other as and when required.

Other responsibilities: typing letters, producing reports.

Working conditions/conditions of service: full time or part time, basic accountancy skills and typing required. Rate of pay £5.00 per hour basic, depending on age, qualifications and experience.

Personal requirements: GCSEs, GCEs, including English Language and Mathematics. RSA II, basic accountancy.

Person specification

Essential	Desirable	Conflicting
Qualifications		
RSA II	Accountancy	
	GCSE maths	
	English language	
Intelligence/aptitudes		
Arithmetical	Verbal	
Personality		
Conscientious	Conforming	Self-indulgent
	Sociable	

<u>Interests</u>

                       Business

<u>Motivation</u>

                       Personal esteem

<u>Appearance/circumstances</u>
Smart appearance

How the review system works

The review system for Street & Co is virtually non-existent, except in the sense of the day-to-day running of the organisation. This consists of informally checking any errors made (through the double-checking system mentioned in the job description), and who makes them. If someone appears to be making 'too many errors' (an undefined quantity) then one of the partners will talk to them to find out why. If one of the accounts preparation clerks has a personal problem that is affecting work, or wishes to discuss anything, the only system that exists is for them to try and catch one of the partners in a free minute.

Clearly, the review system at Street & Co is not very efficient. As it is only a small organisation there is no personnel department as such, nor is there a single person responsible for personnel issues. This needs to be rectified. One (or more) of the partners should take on the responsibility for personnel issues such as recruitment, review and personnel records.

The partner might object that this would take up too much of their valuable time. They need to realise that their employees are valuable too. Once a system is established, it need not take up very much time, perhaps one morning a week at the most. Unfortunately the time taken to set up the system will be quite significant. This is what puts many employers off. If none of the partners can really take time off to organise the new personnel system, then outside help can be obtained in the form of a management consultant, not just any management consultant, but one experienced in personnel issues, especially performance review.

Conclusion

There are a number of key changes to be made at Street & Co. Firstly, employee records and job descriptions need to be organised and kept up to date. The organisation first needs the means of collecting relevant performance data – for accounts clerks this will be number of errors made, speed of working, typing speed, supervisor (partner) ratings. The review system system can then be organised.

A company like this might need regular performance reviews every twelve months, with a constant check kept on performance throughout the year. The regular performance review needs to include:

- target performance
- actual performance
- a discussion of any discrepancies between actual and target performance
- reviewee grievances
- opportunities for self-development
- any other matters.

A review form should be designed to incorporate these sections.

Performance reviews should all be carried out by the partner responsible for personnel issues. All the reviews should be carried out around the same time of year, so that after the results of the interviews have been obtained all the partners can meet to discuss the findings: what training should be offered, whether anyone's duties should be altered, whether the organisation is running smoothly, whether everyone is satisfied with their work, and if not why not.

TECHNICAL MANAGER

The technical manager is 35 years old, and has been working with the company for two years.

Task analysis
Job title: technical manager
Department: technical
Company: Vargenpane
Reviewee's name: Chas Roberts

Task	Knowledge/skills	Aptitudes	Personality
Supervising technical staff	General management skills	Leadership	Self-assured Flexible Assertive
Quality control	Chemistry	Observation	Experimenting
Advising end-users	Product knowledge	Verbal	Sociable
Reporting to MD	Departmental knowledge	Verbal	Self-assured Relaxed
Communicating with other departments		Verbal	Sociable
Internal and external audits	BS5750		Attention to detail
Staff appraisal	Interviewing Counselling	Verbal Numerical	Adaptable Mature
Presentations	Public speaking	Verbal	Confident Relaxed
Product development	Chemistry Consumer	Analytical	Patient Experimenting

This task analysis is necessarily only a summary as the technical manager can be called upon to attend to a very wide variety of tasks, including all those normally carried out by subordinates, in addition to his usual tasks.

Job description
Job title: technical manager.
Department: technical.
Responsible to: managing director.
Responsible for: personal assistant, product development manager, R & D technicians, QC team leader, QC technicians, trainees.
Number employed on this work: 18.

Position from which candidates for this job might come: chemical industry.

Avenues of promotion/transfer from this position: directorship, operations, marketing.

Purposes/objects of work: to co-ordinate and supervise the operation of the technical department.

Main duties/activities: supervisory, customer services, improving existing standards/products, conducting internal and external audits.

Forms/equipment: working procedures, quality manual, quality control specifications, chemistry laboratory equipment.

Contacts: daily, with all departments, suppliers, distributors, end-users.

Discretion: rarely receive written/oral instructions from directors. Methods of work, order of tasks can be varied quite considerably.

Checking: no regular checking. Weekly meeting with MD to discuss work, and any errors made.

Supervision required: none.

Supervision given: responsibility for assigning/checking work, performance assessment, discipline, and dealing with grievances. Involved with recommending appointments, transfers, promotion, and discharges. Can provide performance bonuses within a previously agreed budget.

Other responsibilities: market research of products.

Working conditions/conditions of service: office, staff canteen. £22,000 + car.

Personal requirements: degree in chemistry, managerial and supervisory skills, knowledge of BS5750.

The task analysis and job description have given some idea of the breadth of knowledge and skills required in the job of technical manager, along with some desirable personality traits. The kind of individual that fits the post is determined using the person specification.

Person specification

Essential	Desirable	Conflicting
Qualifications		
Degree in		
Chemistry	Chemical engineering	

Intelligence/aptitudes		
Verbal	Numerical	
Scientific		
Writing		

Personality		
Self-sufficient	Relaxed	Immature
Confident	Attentive	Tender-minded
Leadership	Sociable	Dependent

Interests		
	Practical	
	Administrative	

Motivation		
Dedication	Status	

Appearance/circumstances	
Smart, clean	Nights away

The section with most information is personality. This is because good managers need certain characteristics that enable them not only to be competent at the jobs carried out by their subordinates, but also to have the personal and leadership traits that enable them to succeed.

How the review system works

The review system for Chas is very informal. Basically, it consists of the weekly meeting with the MD mentioned in the job description. There is supposed to be a formal review system in operation, but in the two years he has been there, Chas has never had such a review.

The weekly meeting with the MD is quite thorough as far as the job is concerned. The discussions cover the performance of the department in general, what has been achieved and what needs to be achieved. The meeting acts as a check that the department is acting in line with company policy. Chas himself is not directly reviewed, except in the sense that if there are any mistakes in his department, he is the one who gets the blame.

A 'review' such as this ensures that all departments are kept in touch with company policy (the MD meets all departmental heads individually, once a week), but it does little to help the individual manager. It is implicitly accepted that the meeting will only consider issues of performance, not any problems Chas may be experiencing. If Chas does have a problem, he can't discuss it at the meeting because it 'isn't the right time or place'.

There is clearly a need for a *formal* review system that will take into account the needs of individual managers, not one that is rumoured to exist, but one that actually functions.

The review system for subordinates is at the moment virtually non-existent. Though the company is not small, employing around 250 people, there is no company policy regarding reviews. Each department head is expected to organise his or her own review system. Chas has been trying to do this for some time, but is put off by a number of factors. Firstly, before taking this post he had never expected to do reviews. He had never been trained to do them, he wouldn't have known where to start. In the last two years he has tentatively attempted a few reviews when the need arose. For instance, an opening arose in the marketing department that he thought might suit one of his staff, so he arranged a review meeting with her to discuss her possible transfer to the marketing department. The interview did achieve some success. Chas found out that Caroline was bored in her present job – but she didn't want to go into marketing. Instead, Chas has tried to develop her present post to open up new opportunities. Another review has been arranged for six months' time to see if the new arrangements are working.

Because there is no formal review system, Chas would not otherwise have found out that Caroline was dissatisfied in her present job. She wasn't the type to complain.

Chas has found other obstacles in his way to setting up a review system for the technical department. Because he has no formal knowledge of, or training in, performance review he has contacted other departments which he knows do run reviews to find out what they do. Unfortunately it is very difficult to get information from them. They are always too busy, or shrug it off with a comment like: 'Well, you just interview everyone and ask if they're getting on all right'.

Conclusion
The company would benefit from a systematic performance review system that would include training potential reviewers such as Chas, and encourage formal reviews for all levels of staff.

UNIVERSITY LECTURER

Sue is 41 years old and is in her first year as a lecturer.

Task analysis
Job title: University lecturer
Company: University of Heage
Reviewee's name: Sue Morton
Reviewer's name: Ian Southwell

Task	Knowledge/skills	Aptitudes	Personality
Lecturing	Specialist knowledge of several areas of psychology	Verbal ability Logical thought Structuring information	Sociability Receptive
Personal tutoring	Course structure		Friendly Sympathetic Intuitive
Research	Detailed knowledge of particular areas of psychology	Logical Analytical Writing Lateral thought Attention to detail	Dedication Persistence Patience
Administration	Knowledge of organisational structure	Methodical	
Course development	Structuring Relevance	Delegation	Teamwork

Job description
Job title: senior lecturer.
Company: University of Heage.
Responsible to: head of department.
Responsible for: NA.
Number employed on this work: 20.
Position from which candidates for this job might come: other similar organisations, postgraduate researchers.

Purpose/objects of work: lecturing and tutoring undergraduate students, carrying out original research.

Forms/equipment: books, research papers, course materials, memos.

Contacts: daily contact with students and with other members of lecturing staff.

Discretion: redesign of course materials.

Checking: annual teaching observation, review, mentor system in operation.

Supervision required: some problems with students, ensuring course design acceptable.

Supervision given: students.

Other responsibilities: presenting research papers at conferences, writing for publication.

Working conditions/conditions of service: personal office, shared secretarial service, library, £23,000.

Personal requirements: degree and higher degree in psychology

The task analysis and job description give some idea of the variety in the job and the responsibility the person has. They show that a wide range of abilities and attributes are required of someone who is to be an effective lecturer. A lecturer not only has to lecture, but must be, among other things, a personal advisor, an administrator, a writer; in other words, a good all round communicator.

Person specification

Essential	Desirable	Conflicting
Qualifications		
BSc degree	Teaching qualification	
PhD in psychology		
Intelligence/aptitudes		
High general intelligence	Integrating knowledge	
Verbal		
Logical		
Analytical		
Numerical		

Personality

Dedicated	Sociable	Inability to
Enthusiastic	Maturity	communicate
Questioning		

Interests

| Research | Lecturing |
| Psychology | People |

Motivation

Dedication	Money
Desire for knowledge	
To communicate	
knowledge	
Vocational	

Appearance/circumstances

| Casual | 9–5 worker |

How the review system works

Sue's review system is not one of the most effective. Given that she is in a job that requires such a range of abilities, motivation, etc., the review system is sadly deficient, as it is for many professionals.

The review system in her university, though it has been set up as a standard system for all academics and support staff, is not really taken seriously, either by those who set up the system (as is often the case it was set up by people who have little knowledge of the kind of work carried out by the people the system was 'designed for'), or by those involved in the system.

It is a peer-review system, where each member of staff is reviewed by another member of staff of the same department. In effect this means each person acts as the reviewer and each person as the reviewee. As mentioned in an earlier chapter, this system can be open to abuse, in terms of 'you pat my back, I'll pat yours'. The staff don't really have much of an incentive to carry out effective reviews, firstly because they don't have time and secondly, they have little power to offer, anything, as the head of department, Professor Riser, has difficulties delegating responsibility to other members of staff, preferring to keep personal control of budgets as he finds it difficult to accept that other people can act responsibly.

The system itself is not designed to minimise problems. The

review form consists of a series of very general questions relating to work performance and personal needs, with categories of A and B, where A indicates satisfactory and B unsatisfactory. If B is indicated then there is a secondary process for determining the reasons for the problem and attempting to find solutions, but because this is time-consuming most reviewers simply record A, and most reviewees agree to this, as if they really want something to change they have to approach the head of department.

Sue's appraisal with Ian was very straightforward, taking five minutes to write down the As and twenty minutes to discuss departmental gossip. Ian then sent one copy of the form to personnel, a second to the head of department, a third to Sue, and kept the fourth.

Conclusion

The system here needs fairly radical change, the first requirement being to attempt to change it in the eyes of the staff. The review has little value unless something positive can come out of it. In order for this to happen, simple A or B grading is not enough and, more importantly, the reviewer and the reviewee need more power to provide the reviewee with things that are judged to be required. Two fundamental changes would help:

- Alter the review form to include more detail.

- The head of department must delegate more power to the reviewer.

SUPERMARKET CASHIER

Gillian is 30 years old and has worked as a cashier for five years.

Task analysis

Job title: cashier
Company: Betterbuys
Reviewee's name: Gillian Rose
Supervisor's name: Kevin Lesley

Task	Knowledge/skills	Aptitudes	Personality
Till operating	Till operations	Numerical	Pleasant
	Cheque handling		Polite

	Returns/refunds		Helpful Relaxed
Shelf filling			
Stocktaking	Numeracy/literacy		Attention to detail
Weighing fruit/veg			
Serving on food counter	Types of food	Judging weights	Friendly disposition

Job description
Job title: cashier.

Company: Betterbuys.

Responsible to: checkout supervisor.

Responsible for: NA.

Number employed on this work: 23.

Position from which candidates for this job might come: external.

Avenues of promotion/transfer from this position: checkout supervisor.

Purpose/objects of work: to serve customers.

Main duties/activities: operating till, stocking shelves, serving on food counter, weighing fruit/vegetables, stocktaking.

Forms/equipment: checkout tills, refund forms, stock inventories, weighing scales.

Contacts: regular daily contact with: supervisor, manager, customers, other cashiers.

Discretion: little scope to vary methods of work. Oral instructions from supervisor and manager.

Checking: till receipts checked daily.

Supervision required: on tills, all difficulties referred to supervisor, including wrongly priced goods, unpriced goods, problems with tills, cheques, alcohol (if cashier under 18).

Supervision given: none.

Other responsibilities: responding to customer enquiries.

Working conditions/conditions of service: shifts varied between 0800–2000. Basic pay, £4.00 an hour (trained), overtime available. Part-time or full-time. Staff canteen.

Personal requirements: basic literacy/numeracy, cleanliness, smart appearance, cheerful disposition.

Person specification

Essential	Desirable	Conflicting
Qualifications		
	GCSE Maths/English	
Intelligence/aptitudes		
	Numerical	
Personality		
Friendly, honest, polite, helpful		Aggressive
Interests		
	People	
Motivation		
		Status
Appearance/circumstances		
Clean, smart		

How the review system works

The cashiers at Betterbuys have a reasonably good review system. They all join as trainees, usually for six months, during which time they are trained in all the tasks involved, under close supervision. At the end of this period they are reviewed. This has two aims, to ensure they are happy with their work before being promoted to fully-trained cashier, and to ensure they are doing well at all tasks.

There is also a regular performance review every year. This is the responsibility of one of the assistant managers. The purposes are to consider the reviewee's performance, their own feelings about the job, and their potential for promotion.

Performance data consist of a written report from the supervisor and error rates on the till receipts.

Gillian's last review showed her performance to be excellent, with consistently good supervisor reports. The management wanted her to apply for a supervisor's position. At the review interview Gillian felt rather pressured, and though she didn't want the job she applied for it and got it. It quickly went wrong. She found the new responsibility difficult, and after only four months asked to go back to her previous job.

Conclusion

This illustration shows the importance of carrying out reviews properly. The reviewer made the basic mistake of assuming that someone who was good at one job would be good at another one. The promotion review should have included an assessment of Gillian's potential as a supervisor, particularly her potential for taking responsibility. The reviewer should have been wary from the start as she didn't really want the job in the first place.

SUGGESTED PROJECTS

1. Design a review procedure for the accounts preparation clerk.

2. Design a review procedure for the technical manager.

3. Take an example of the way you currently review an individual, or the way you are reviewed yourself, and put it in the format of the above case studies. Highlight the problems or potential problems with the procedure.

Glossary

Aptitude. An ability relating to a specific task or area of knowledge to do with the job (e.g. sales aptitude, mechanical aptitude).

Bias. Acting more favourably towards one person or group than another without good reason. Bias can arise in the individual or be an integral part of the review system (i.e. biased interviewer or biased data). Simply having the knowledge that bias exists can help reduce its effects. Validation of the review system should determine how much bias exists. It is crucial to try and avoid bias, though this is sometimes very difficult, both because much of the data collected relating to many jobs is subjective, and also because many reviewers and reviewees know each other and work together on a day-to-day basis.

Career development. One primary aim of the review for reviewees is to ensure that their future within the organisation is being properly planned, that it is going in the right direction. Performance review is an opportunityfor individuals to express any dissatisfaction and to suggest alternative courses of action (e.g. transfer or retraining).

Communication. The act of conveying information between two parties. Effective communication in the review interview is essential. All relevant information should be received at the right time by both parties, whether verbal or written.

Conflict. Conflict or opposition is unavoidable in many reviews, whether it is related to the job, e.g. how it is being done, or to the person, e.g. whether the two parties get on well together. The word 'opposition' implies that two parties have separate ideas and, for whatever reason, fail to communicate.

Correlation. A statistical technique used to determine the degree of relationship or association between two variables. The closer the relationship, the higher the correlation. A perfect positive correlation is represented by +1.0, a perfect negative correlation by -1.0. If there is no relationship at all, this is represented by 0.0.

Counselling. Counselling is being used by more and more organisations as they recognise it has a number of essential puposes, from reducing stress to the analysis of personal problems. Counselling involves listening to the individual, empathising with their situation and helping them to work through their problem in their own way.

Data (quantitative/qualitative). Data are the information collected for use in the review. Quantitative data are numerical data, perhaps in the form of rating scales or psychometric test results. Qualitative data are usually in verbal or written form. They are non-quantifiable. Both kinds of data are open to bias and problems of interpretation if not used carefully.

Discrimination. This refers to the differential treatment of groups of people, with prejudicial connotations. Society is still having difficulty ridding itself of the various kinds of discrimination, for example race, sex, sexual preferences, age. It is important that the reviewer does not introduce bias in the review system through discrimination. Apart from being unethical and diminishing the validity of the system, it may also be illegal.

Feedback. The reviewee should receive information relating to their performance not just after the review interview, but throughout the year. Feedback should be constructive, and should consider where performance is good (praise/reward) as well as poor (criticism/ punishment).

Follow up. The concrete results of the review, specifically where decisions are made to take action of one sort or another (training/transfer, etc.).

Future potential. What is the individual likely to achieve in the future? In which areas are they likely to be successful? A review to assess future potential is often carried out shortly after an individual joins the organisation to see how to best satisfy both individual and organisational needs.

Intelligence. General mental ability, as opposed to specific attitudes. Psychologists define intelligence in terms of the ability to adapt effectively to novel situations. Intelligence is not concerned with the individual's particular knowledge and skills, but with the general ability to carry out a range of tasks. The measurement of intelligence (often known as IQ or intelligence quotient) can predict performance in many situations.

Interview. Interviewing is used in any situation where people wish to receive and give verbal information in an orderly fashion.

Interviews can be one-to-one, as in most reviews, or many-to-one (or panel) as is the case for many selection interviews.

Interviewing skills. The success or otherwise of the interview depends on the type of questions asked and the responses they elicit. Interviewers should give a lot of thought to the questions they will ask in the interview, and ask questions that are going to produce the most information without distressing the interviewee. The interviewee should similarly prepare for the interview, both by preparing answers to questions they think they will be asked, and by thinking of some questions they themselves wish to ask.

Job analysis. A job is dissected into its component parts using task analyses, interviews with staff, personnel and job records, to determine the structure of the job. The job needs to be fully understood when designing a review system.

Job description. All jobs should provide an accurate, detailed, and up-to-date job description so workers are clear about their duties and responsibilities. The job description should make the job-holder's position and responsibilities within the organisation clear.

Job redesign. This involves restructuring the job, perhaps after problems have emerged through job analysis. Tasks may be altered, added or removed in order to create a more coherent structure and maximise the efficiency and satisfaction of workers carrying out the job. It should be carried out in consultation with job-holders, supervisors, and anyone else involved in the job.

Job satisfaction. In previous decades, organisations have focused on maximising productivity. Now they are more likely to emphasise the welfare of the employee. This in turn benefits the organisation. If individuals are to give their best, they should have satisfaction in the job.

Leadership. Leadership is crucial to organisational success. The best leaders share certain personal qualities; they tend on the whole to be sociable, extrovert, considerate towards others, assertive and intuitive. They are not necessarily more intelligent than the rest of the team, but they can create and maintain group cohesion and give direction and purpose to group activities. But effective leadership is more than having the right personal qualities, the ethos of the organisation is also important.

Listening skills. These are crucial to any interviewer, and anyone involved with counselling (i.e. all reviewers). The person doing the listening must be active and genuine, that is, they should empathise with the speaker and make appropriate comments.

Motivation. The 'whys' behind people's actions. People behave in certain ways because they have certain needs. These can be basic physiological needs such as the need for food, warmth and shelter, or psychological needs such as companionship and personal growth. In the work environment it is mainly the psychological needs that require attention as the state largely provides for physiological needs.

Negotiation. Or bargaining. Negotiation concerns the rules of discussion that are involved when two people with differing initial positions try to reach a compromise acceptable to both.

Objectives/targets. Employees perform better when they know what to try and achieve. Targets are often difficult to set. They can be difficult to quantify (especially for managers), or difficult to set at a reasonable level, one neither impossible nor too easy to reach, both of which will demotivate the reviewee.

Peer ratings. These are gaining in popularity though they must be used with caution. They arose because individuals who work together know a great deal about each other's performance. Clearly, they should be used with care. They must be anonymous and confidential. There is the danger that some people might indulge in backbiting and the airing of personal grievances, and try to put each other down in order to show themselves in a better light.

Performance criteria. Some jobs have performance criteria that are simple to determine, e.g. number of components manufactured in one hour. Others are more difficult, e.g. the effectiveness of the marketing manager. Whatever the criteria used, it is desirable to choose ones that are not biased. If they are quantifiable, all the better.

Performance review The process of estimating the value of an individual to the organisation and vice versa through regular assessment. There are a number of purposes of review, including reviewing performance, assessing training needs and making future plans. Apart from assessing how well the individual meets the needs of the organisation, the review should be assessing the organisation to determine how well it meets the needs of the individual.

Person specification. The theorectically ideal individual for a particular job. The specification includes particular categories, such as intelligence, aptitudes, personality. These are derived from the job description and from the individuals who already do the job.

Personality. Relatively permanent ways of behaving which characterise individuals and make them different from others. The differences are called 'traits', e.g. extroversion, aggression, honesty. Personality, when measured accurately, can be a predictor of job success, and is useful for assessing training needs.

Psychometric testing. Psychometric tests and questionnaires can provide detailed, objective information on abilities, personality and interests very quickly. Tests are accurate predictors of how an individual will perform in various circumstances. For example, they are a particularly useful form of data in reviews relating to future performance in other roles (promotion/transfer).

Reliability. Any assessment device (e.g. psychometric test, interview, appraisal system as a whole) should produce consistent, stable findings if used to measure the same thing on two or more occasions.

Reviewer The individual carrying out the review. This role can be fulfilled by the line manager, the supervisor, or a specialist from the personnel department.

Selection. Job selection is concerned with picking the right person for the job. Many of the principles of performance review as outlined in this book apply equally to selection, for instance the need to have accurate and up-to-date job descriptions and person specifications, and ways of accurately assessing candidates on important individual characteristics.

Subordinate ratings. These are an alternative to supervisor ratings, though they may present difficulties and should only be used with care. It is unlikely that subordinates actually know enough about the role of the supervisor to make valid judgements about performance. For this reason, it is usually best to restrict subordinate ratings to areas such as judgement of leadership and social interaction skills.

Supervisor. This broad term means anyone responsible for a group of people (or even a single person) in an organisation. The notion of authority is difficult to assess. In some circumstances the supervisor has a great deal of authority (for example, hiring and firing, discipline), in others very little.

Supervisor ratings. One of the commonest forms of data used in performance review. They are also one of the most abused assessment techniques. Supervisor ratings scales are often devised without much thought. On the other hand, carefully designed scales provide useful and valid information.

Task analysis. Part of job analysis. The task analysis determines the number and types of tasks involved in the job, the frequency with which they are carried out, and the percentage of time spent on the task.

Training. This is one of the most important outcomes of performance review. The analysis of training needs is a crucial part of many reviews. There is little point in finding out a person's deficiencies if this information isn't acted on, and acted on quickly. The costs of training are usually quickly recouped.

Validation. A good review system will always have defects due to its complexity. Validation is a form of systematic analysis involving experimental analysis of the system, interviews with the individuals involved, etc., to discover any defects and to find ways of remedying them. Its basic purpose is to minimise the defects.

Validity. The extent to which something (e.g. the review system, an interview, supervisor ratings) is accurate (is it measuring what it is supposed to measure?) and useful (does it measure or predict performance?) in a particular situation. Validity is often assessed using correlations. A correlation of 1.0 represents perfect validity, while 0.0 represents no validity.

Further Reading

Conducting Effective Interviews, Ann Dobson (How To Books, 1996).

Effective Performance Appraisals, Robert Maddux (Kogan Page, 1987). A brief introductory guide to the subject. Paperback.

How to Employ & Manage Staff, Wendy Wyatt (How To Books, 2nd edition 1995). A practical handbook covering both management practice and the legal requirements of employment statutes and regulations.

Writing a Report, John Bowden (How To Books, 4th edition 1995). A systematic guide to management report writing and presentation.

Making Performance Appraisals Work, Tom Philp (McGraw-Hill, 1983).

The Secrets of Successful Staff Appraisal and Counselling, Clive Goodworth (Heinemann, 1989).

Performance Appraisal and Career Development, Clive Fletcher & Richard Williams (Hutchinson, 1985). A more detailed and academic study.

Index